How Steam Locomotives Work

Brian Solomon

Dedication:
To the Memory of Thomas M. Hoover

Kalmbach Media
21027 Crossroads Circle
Waukesha, Wisconsin 53186
www.KalmbachHobbyStore.com

Published in 2022
26 25 24 23 22 2 3 4 5 6

Manufactured in China

ISBN: 978-1-62700-880-8
EISBN: 978-1-62700-881-5

Editor: Jeff Wilson
Book Design: Lisa Schroeder

Library of Congress Control Number: 2021947513

On the cover: A Pennsylvania Railroad class I1s 2-10-0 gets its train underway at Max Siding on the railroad's Elmira Branch near Trout Run, Pa., on May 4, 1957.
Jim Shaughnessy; collection of the Center for Railroad Photography and Art

Back cover: Crew members oil rod and axle bearings on a Central Vermont 4-8-2 during a station stop at White River Junction, Vt., in June 1950.
Jim Shaughnessy; collection of the Center for Railroad Photography and Art

Contents

Acknowledgements

The steam era ended before I was born. Yet, the culture of the steam locomotive lives on. From the time I could stand I've been observing the railroad. My earliest experiences with steam locomotives at work stem from visits with my family to Steamtown in Bellows Falls, Vt., and climbing on Boston & Maine 3713, a Lima-built Pacific displayed in front of the Boston Museum of Science. Years later I learned that this engine was also part of the Steamtown collection. As a youngster, I wondered, what was this dinosaur and how did work?

A kid's book featuring drawings of a locomotive's interior workings captured my fascination: this showed a fire ablaze inside the firebox, and illustrated internal workings in color. My father, Richard Jay Solomon, has had the privilege of experiencing and photographing steam locomotives in their final years. Through his photographs, I was able to see into a world that ended before my time. Robert A. Buck, proprietor of Tucker's Hobbies in Warren, Mass., was a conduit for my interest. His vast collection of photographs and steam-era literature taught me about steam, and several of his photographs appear in this book. Bob introduced me to many railroaders and steam enthusiasts; among them was Stuart Woolley, a retired Boston & Albany fireman, George C. Corey, a long-time friend and steam photographer, and the late Harry Vallas, who entertained my curiosity on the workings of locomotive valve gear.

In the 1990s I had the opportunity to speak with many members of the steam fraternity through my work at Pentrex Publishing, and in 1996, Motorbooks' Lee Klancher contracted me to write *The American Steam Locomotive,* which sent me on a more focused journey to research and photograph steam locomotives. During the course of this project, John P. Hankey made numerous connections for me while providing valuable history lessons, while John and Dick Gruber offered countless introductions to the steam fraternity, and accompanied me on various occasions to witness steam in action.

Thanks to the many steam people over the years at museums and tourist railways in the United States and abroad who have answered my questions and allowed me to experience live steam locomotives in motion. After I began work on this project, I accepted a full-time job at Conway Scenic Railroad as the manager of Marketing and Events, which allowed me opportunities to experience the operation of the railroad's 0-6-0 no. 7470 and gain a better understanding of its workings. Special thanks to Conway Scenic's Dave Swirk, Louis Edmonds, and the shop crew.

Special thanks to Pat Yough for his help in making and finding photographs; to Vic and Becky Stone for trips to photograph Norfolk & Western 611; Brian Jennison and J.D. Schmid for opportunities to photograph Southern Pacific and Union Pacific steam; and Paul Hammond at the California State Railroad Museum. Kurt Bell, a professional archivist at the State Archives in Harrisburg, opened many doors over the years and lent his enthusiasm to my projects. Bill Keay has helped with my quest for history, especially regarding New England railroading. The members of the Irish Railway Record Society in Dublin have generously given me access to their vast resource of railway literature, while the Railway Preservation Society of Ireland has allowed me a more thorough understanding of steam locomotive workings. Special thanks to the late Tony Renehan for a better understanding of steam locomotive operation. John H. White Jr., offered me perspective on various aspects of 19th century steam.

Photographers who participated are each credited by their images. Thanks to Parsons Witbeck Clark for giving me access to her father, Robert A. Witbeck's, exceptional photographs, and to Kenneth Buck for the Robert A. Buck archive. Thanks to Scott Lothes of the Center for Railroad Photography & Art in Madison, Wis., for permissions. Thanks to my mother, Maureen, my brother Sean, and my fiancé, Kris Sabbatino, for their enthusiasm and continuing support, and to my cousin Stella who traveled with me to photograph Santa Fe 3751 at work.

The voluminous body of literature consulted for this project is listed in the bibliography. A few sources stand above the others in their ability to lend information or convey an understanding of the locomotive: Alfred Bruce's *The Steam Locomotive in America,* Matthias Forney's *Catechism of the Locomotive,* Angus Sinclair's *Development of the Locomotive Engine,* Frank M. Swengel's *The American Steam Locomotive: Volume 1, Evolution,* and John H. White's authoritative locomotive books.

Thanks to Jeff Wilson and everyone else at Kalmbach for their roles in transforming my words into the book that you now hold in your hands.

Brian Solomon
North Conway, N.H., June 2021

Baldwin built this 4-8-0 for Norfolk & Western in 1906. This timeless view shows it operating as a rolling museum piece on the Strasburg Rail Road in the 2000s.
Brian Solomon

Steam's mystique

The locomotive departs the station with bell ringing, a blast from the whistle, and a hiss of steam and sharp bark from the stack. In its wake is the scent of coal smoke. As it recedes in the distance, the beat of the engine rapidly picks up pace, and with each stroke the bark tempers ever so slightly.

The steam engine was one of the greatest developments of the industrial revolution, and its transformation from a stationary power plant to a locomotive forever changed transport. The steam engine is an external-combustion design; it converts fuel and water into steam for power in the form of back-and-forth motion, then to rotary motion.

Through adaptation of the steam locomotive, railways connected cities and towns across the nation. The railway shortened the effective distance between population centers, facilitated the rapid growth of industry, and allowed unprecedented rapid settlement of the North American continent.

Britain originated the basic successful design for the steam locomotive, and in the late 1820s and 1830s, British imported engines dominated rapidly emerging American railways. Soon American manufacturers learned to emulate and adapt the steam locomotive. While American locomotive development was parallel with that in Britain and elsewhere, U.S. design rapidly embraced distinctive characteristics. By 1900 what really set American locomotives apart was their size: they grew more quickly and became much larger than those anywhere else in the world. Despite their size, with the exception of a few peculiar experimental engines such as steam-turbine-electrics and some industrial service engines with geared drive, the vast majority of U.S. locomotives followed the reciprocating design of the early British engines.

But what made them go? How did they work? In an age of computerized worldwide mass communications, interstate highways, and intercontinental jet travel, the workings of the steam locomotive may seem like a Byzantine puzzle. And this book aims to solve this puzzle for you!

Chapter 1

Steam locomotive history and basic operation

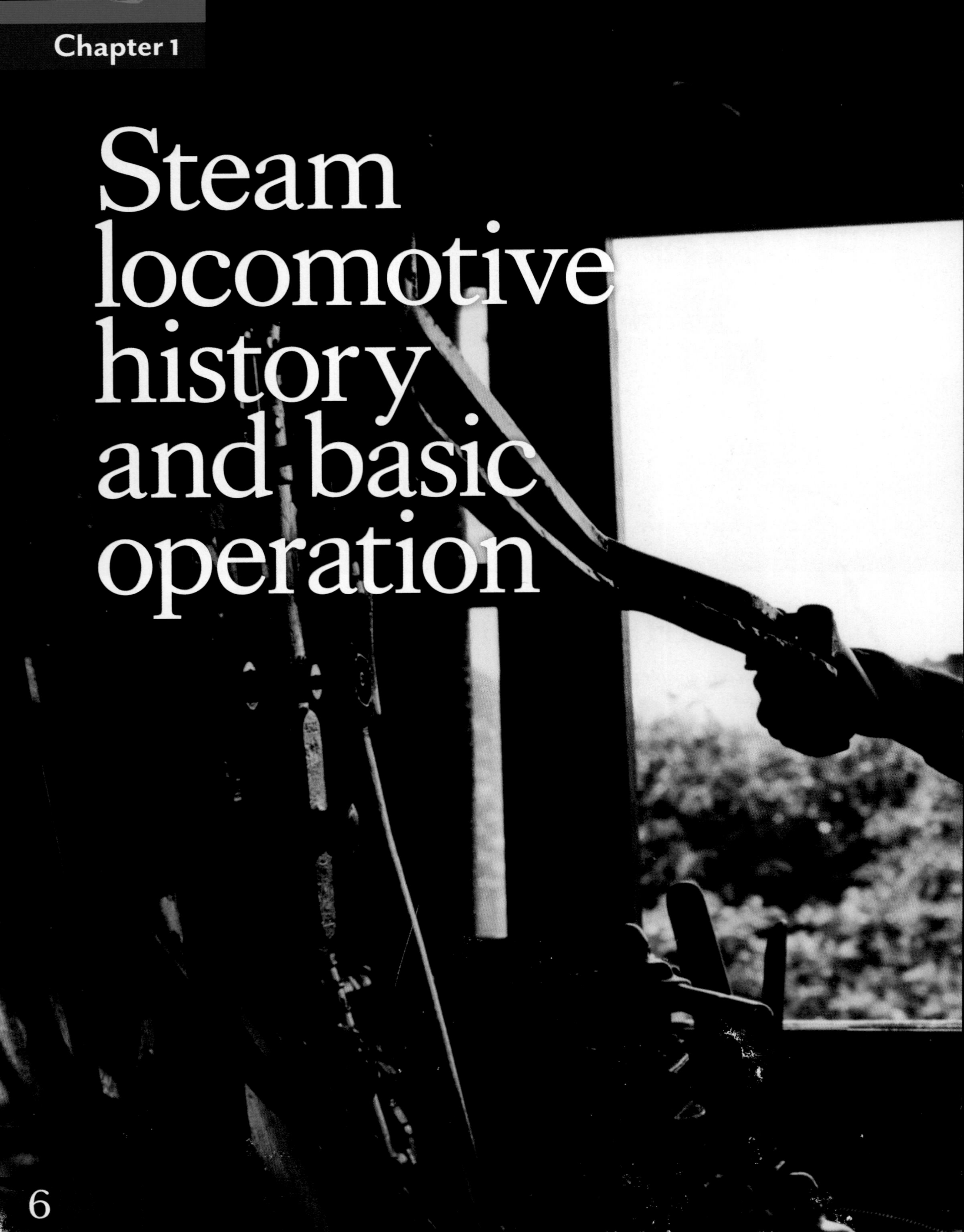

In a classic pose, engineer Walter Dove has his eyes forward, his right hand on the throttle, and his left hand raised to pull the whistle cord of Southern Railway 2-8-2 4501 in 1966. The engineer has a number of controls within reach of his right-hand-side seat; the reverser handle is visible, silhouetted in the lower-left corner of the window. *John Gruber, collection of the Center for Railroad Photography & Art*

The steam engine is a simple external-combustion heat engine. Through the process of combustion it converts fuel to energy by heating water and turning it to steam; through the medium of steam it converts energy into work. A steam locomotive is a steam engine that's designed to convert energy into rotary motion to turn wheels, which propel the locomotive and pull a train.

The steam locomotive was developed in Britain during the first decades of the 19th century. A number of inventors experimented with concepts and developed plans for locomotives, most of which were impractical and didn't work well. Among the first to produce a practical locomotive was George Stephenson, who introduced his first successful locomotive by 1815. Further refinements by George and his son Robert established technological precedents that prevailed for the next century and half.

Robert Stephenson's experimental locomotive *Rocket,* built in 1829, was the first to incorporate the three essential elements that established the common configuration used by the vast majority of

Steam locomotives are powerful machines. Modern steam locomotives could pull mile-long freight trains, carry passengers at 100 miles an hour, and conquer steep mountain grades. Here Union Pacific 4-8-4 no. 825 leads a hotshot mail and express train. The UP used number boards to indicate train numbers—in this case, the second section of Train 6, the *Fast Mail*. The locomotive was built by Alco in 1939. *Robert A. Witbeck, collection of the Center for Railroad Photography & Art*

subsequent successful steam locomotive designs: a horizontal multi-tubular (fire-tube) boiler, a forced draft from cylinder exhaust, and direct connections between the cylinders and driving wheels using rods and crankpins. Although none of these three elements were unique to the *Rocket,* it was the first to combine them in a simple manner that made it superior to all previous locomotives.

The basic engine arrangement, known as the Stephenson Cycle, established an automatic relationship between the rate of fuel combustion with the demand for steam used by the cylinders. Even though the size of individual locomotives, the materials used for construction, and the specific arrangements of cylinders have varied among different designs, the essence of the Stephenson engine has remained unchanged.

Variations in design were implemented as a means to apply the locomotive to specific applications as well as to improve output, efficiency, and reliability. The great numbers of individual designs were a reflection of the locomotive's inherent limitations including the need to carry its fuel, the characteristics of different railway lines (such as clearance restrictions, grades, train weight, and desired speeds), the direct connection between pistons and running gear, and myriad efforts to improve the efficiency of the engine.

Design variations and specifics of various locomotive components will be discussed in detail throughout this book. We'll begin with a look at the steam locomotive's most basic elements and functions, saving the details for later.

Basic arrangement

The basic standard equipment arrangement has been applied to locomotives ranging in size from diminutive four-wheel industrial engines to gargantuan articulated double-engines measuring 118 feet long and weighing 386 tons.

Since the combustion of fuel and evaporation of water provide the sole means of propulsion, the boiler is of paramount importance. A boiler consists of a firebox, flues and firetubes, steam dome, and a smokebox. The firebox is almost always located at the rear of the boiler, but the style, construction, and size of fireboxes have varied greatly between different engines, and will be the subject of detailed discussion later. The details of boiler construction have filled books with seemingly innumerable variations on the basic equipment.

Robert Stephenson's *Rocket* of 1829 (top) is credited with pioneering the basic arrangement of future steam locomotives, including horizontal boiler, connection from piston rods to driving wheels, and a forced draft created by cylinder exhaust. *Trains magazine collection*

Delaware & Hudson's original *Stourbridge Lion* was built in Britain in 1828 (bottom). In 1829, its test was credited as the first commercial steam locomotive operated in America. This replica was built in 1933. *Library of Congress*

By the mid-1800s, locomotives—although small by 1900s standards—were taking the basic shape and design they would carry throughout the steam era. The Great Northern's *William Crooks* was originally built in 1861 and rebuilt in 1868; following its retirement it was again rebuilt and returned to exhibition service in 1908. James J. Hill, owner of the GN, poses with the locomotive and its crew in 1908. *Great Northern*

Cylinders containing double-acting reciprocating pistons (steam acting alternately on both piston faces) maximize power output by doubling the number of power impulses during each piston cycle. The pistons power driving wheels through a series of direct linkages consisting of a piston rod powering a crosshead (supported by crosshead guides) that acts as the hinged pivot connection to the main rod, which drives a crankpin on a main drive wheel. Side rods transmit the piston thrust when two or more sets of drive wheels (drivers) are employed.

A key to the successful operation of the locomotive is the control of steam admission to the cylinders and its subsequent exhaust, made possible by valves that are regulated by equipment called valve gear. The valve gear is synchronized mechanically to the reciprocating engine and adjusted by the engineer to regulate the length of steam admission during the course of the piston stroke. This function is crucial to the whole operation of the engine, as it serves a function comparable to a transmission in an automobile, and thus allows the engineer to regulate both the direction and the speed of the locomotive. Over the years dozens of valve gear arrangements have been employed, and the details on how some of the more common types function will be discussed in chapter 3.

In addition to the fundamental components are an array of other supplementary apparatus not required for

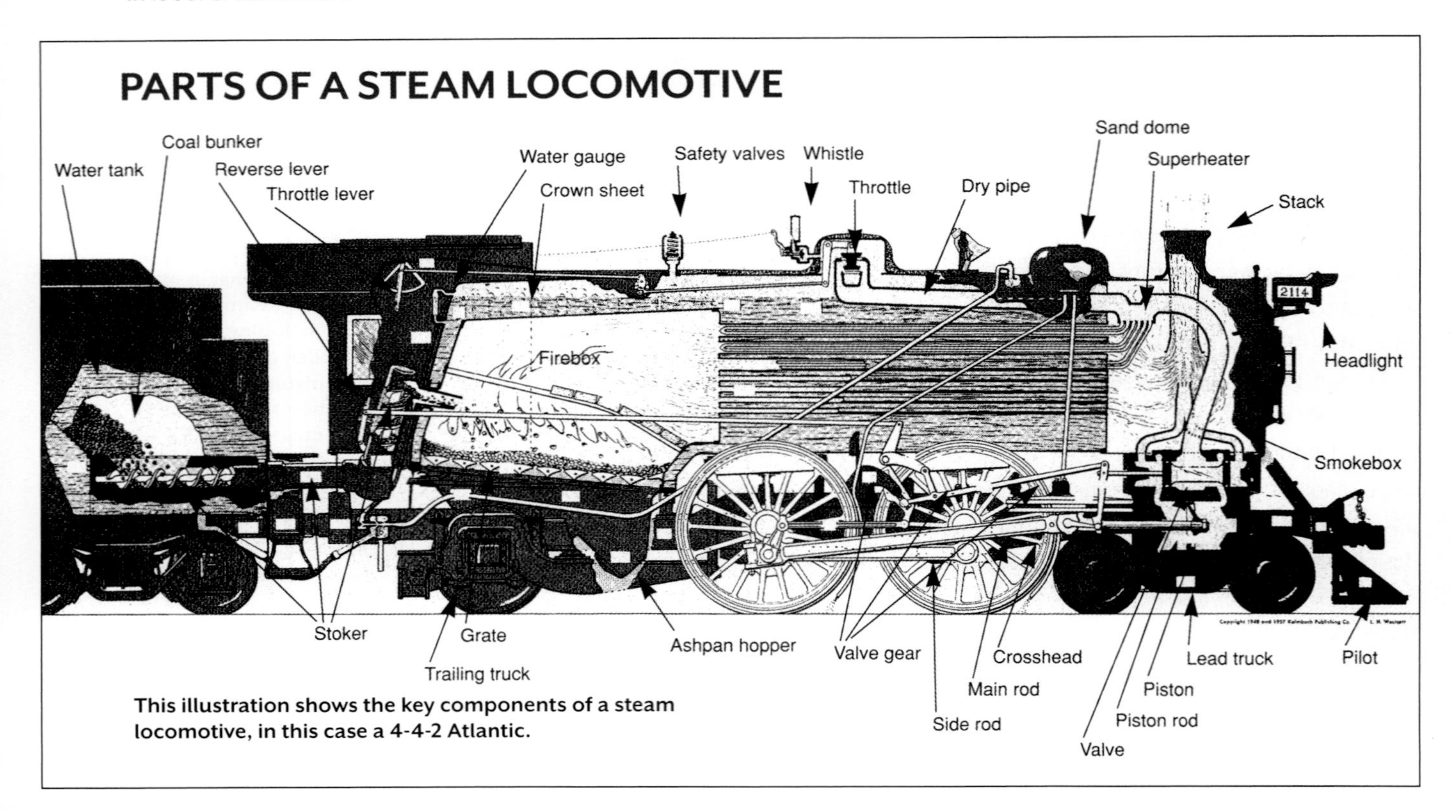

This illustration shows the key components of a steam locomotive, in this case a 4-4-2 Atlantic.

BACKHEAD

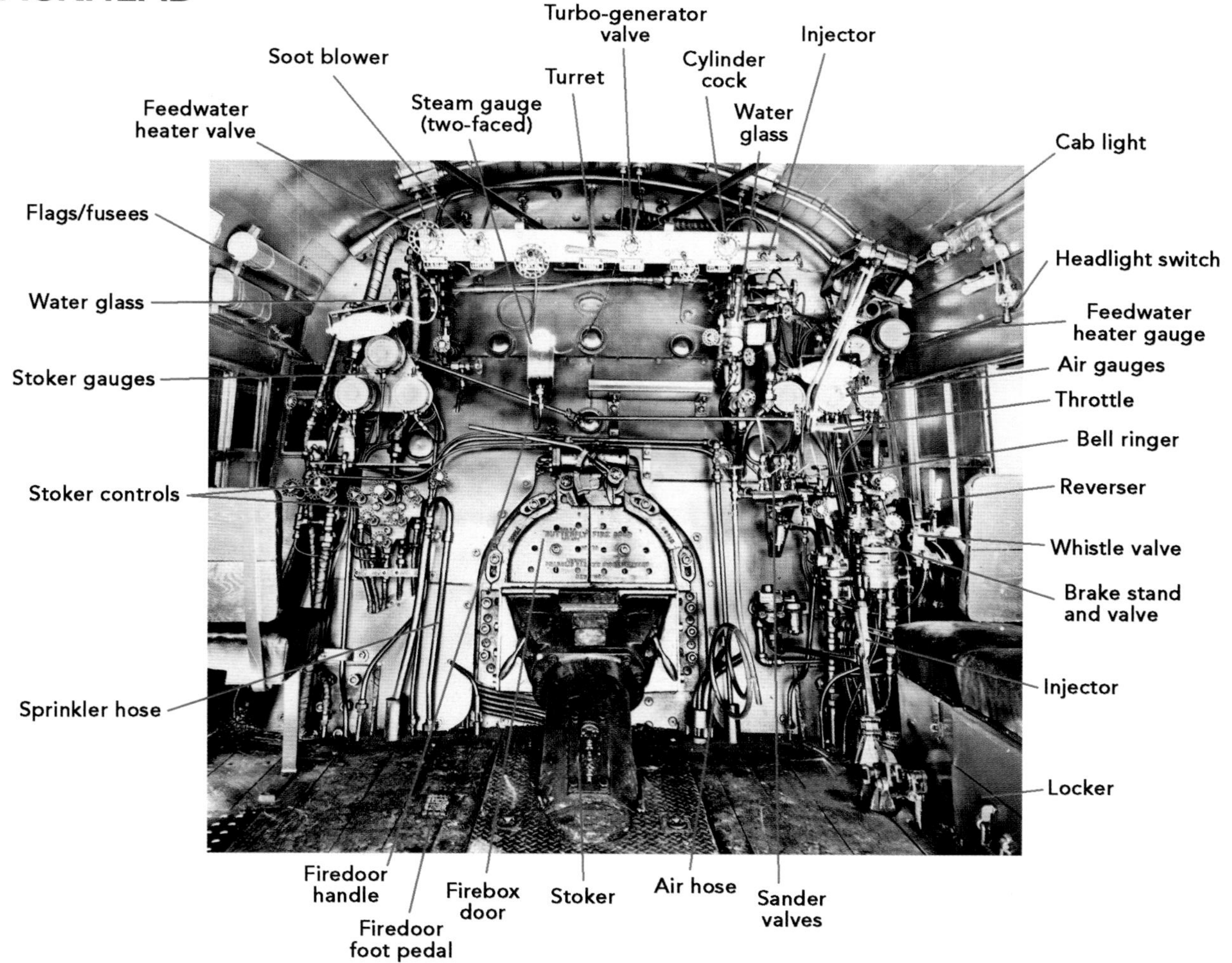

basic motion, but necessary for the machine to function as a railway locomotive. These include braking systems to check and stop the locomotive once in motion; sanding systems to improve adhesion; bells, whistles, and lights to warn and signal people; and various appliances designed to improve the engine's thermal efficiency, including feedwater heaters, superheaters, and lubrication devices.

Basics of operation

The comparison between a steam locomotive and a draft animal is more than merely a romantic idealization. Unlike many modern machines powered by electricity or internal combustion engines, a steam engine cannot be simply switched on or off. Quite the contrary, preparing the engine for service takes hours, and when the work is done, the engine requires routine maintenance before it can be left alone again.

The engine uses a well-tended fire to convert a large volume of water into steam, which is stored under high pressure in the boiler. This steam is gradually released into the cylinders under pressure, where it expands to act upon the pistons. Once used, the steam is finally exhausted through an exhaust nozzle to the stack and upward into the atmosphere.

A typical boiler is a longitudinal barrel, with the lower 70 percent of its volume devoted to water heating area and the top 30 percent for steam storage. Unheated water is stored in a trailing tender—also used for fuel storage—or, on some locomotives, in

Controls and gauges are located on the back-head, the rear of the boiler that protrudes into the front of the cab. The engineer sits on the right and the fireman on the left. *Trains magazine collection*

Visibility can be a challenge in running a steam locomotive, especially when operating in reverse. Here the engineer of restored Chicago & North Western 4-6-0 no. 1385 is in an uncomfortable position. Not only is the throttle control, brake valves and other equipment harder to reach, but he must do his best to get a clear view beyond the tender by leaning out of the cab window. *Brian Solomon*

Firing up a steam locomotive is far more extensive than throwing a switch. Following repairs to this Union Pacific locomotive, its boiler was fed preheated steam to raise the pressure to 140 pounds. This laborer then put a light bed of coal and kindling in the firebox, and has lighted a clump of cotton waste to start the fire. *Union Pacific*

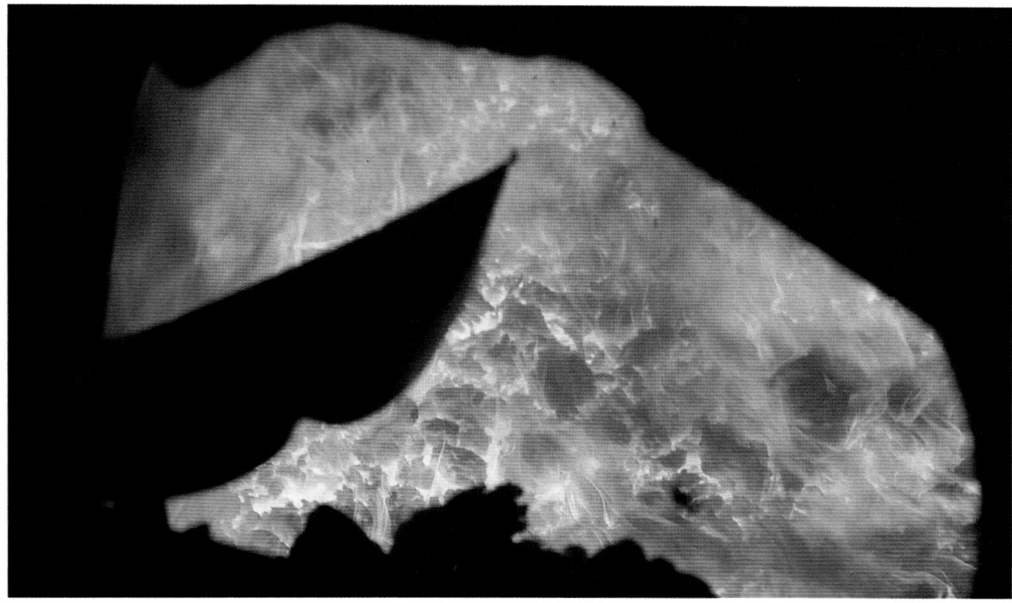

The fireman has the responsibility not only to deliver coal to the firebox, but to direct it to the best places possible to generate the necessary volume of steam in the most efficient means possible. Poor firing technique may result in a waste of coal, a dying or ineffective fire, clinkers, and other problems.
Above: Oren B. Helbok; Left: Brian Solomon

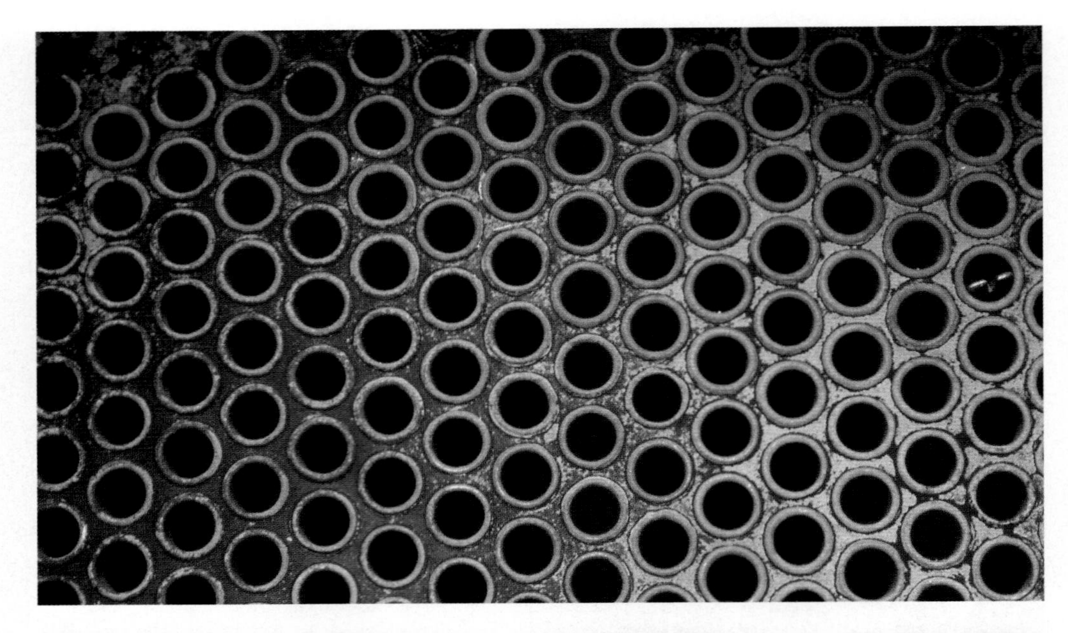

Here's a smokebox-end view of freshly cleaned fire tubes inside a locomotive boiler. Draft from exhaust in the smokebox draws gases from the firebox through the fire tubes. This helps heat the boiler water, which surrounds the tubes. The ends of the fire tubes and flues are held by the flue sheet. *Brian Solomon*

Shopmen inside the smokebox are repairing and cleaning the flue sheet on a Southern Pacific locomotive at the company's Sacramento (Calif.) shops. The flues on superheated locomotives, such as this one, are the larger-diameter openings that house superheater elements; the smaller openings hold fire tubes. Here the flues, tubes, and superheaters have been removed as part of the locomotive's overhaul. *Southern Pacific*

Removing ashes from the locomotive was a daily part of locomotive maintenance. In February 1957, a Pennsylvania Railroad hostler at South Amboy, N.J. cleans the ash pan on K4s Pacific no. 612 using an air line attached to the engine. *Don Wood*

specially designed engine-mounted tanks (thus defining a "tank engine"). Water is introduced to the boiler using one of several devices. Early locomotives used a pump, while later engine designs used steam injectors and feedwater heaters (described in detail later).

A fire is built inside the firebox, which is surrounded by the back of the boiler. Typically the firebox is rectangular in shape (although some early locomotives used hemispherical fireboxes). Flues and firetubes extend from the firebox through the lower portion of the boiler to the smokebox. The number and diameter of these tubes varies depending on the size of the locomotive. Flues are generally larger than firetubes, and in late-era locomotives may contain superheater elements (see Chapter 2).

The fire, tended by the fireman,

40

A crewman uses pressurized water to purge ashes from the ashpans on Valley Railroad no. 40, a tourist-line locomotive in Connecticut. On the ground below the firebox is a growing accumulation of ash.
Brian Solomon

This rear view of the boiler and firebox of Pennsylvania Railroad K4s Pacific 1361 provides a good illustration of the boxy Belpaire firebox design (more on those in Chapter 2). Notice that new stay bolts have been installed on the sides of the firebox. The locomotive is undergoing restoration at Steamtown in Scranton, Pa.
Brian Solomon

gradually heats the water and makes steam. The fire is shaped and banked to ensure the most efficient burning of fuel—control of the locomotive fire is an art. The firebox arrangement depends on the type of fuel burned, and the fireman had a constant balancing act to maximize the use of fuel while avoiding damage to the locomotive.

Steam

Steam engines are very powerful because boiling water has a great deal of latent power. Steam forms and expands to a 1,700:1 ratio when water is heated to its 212-degree (F) boiling point. In an open container—such as a teakettle being heated on a stove—the steam formed when water boils simply flashes to the atmosphere. Steam is invisible: What we see (and often call "steam") is water vapor (tiny droplets) that forms as the steam cools back below the boiling point and condenses. (This condensed moisture can cause serious problems for locomotives; more on that in future chapters.)

To harness steam's energy, a locomotive's boiler is a pressure vessel, keeping the water in liquid form above 212 degrees, creating superheated water—for example, at 200 pounds of pressure, water boils at 381 degrees F. The higher the boiler pressure, the higher the water's boiling point, and the more latent/stored energy that exists. Locomotives in the late 1800s typically operated at pressures of 150 to 175 pounds; by the early 1900s pressures to 200 and 250 pounds were common, with many modern steam locomotives operating at 300 pounds.

This superheated water flashes to steam as pressure is released. It's critical that this be done in a controlled manner, to the cylinders; an uncontrolled release (as when a boiler fails) can result in a catastrophic explosion, as all of the superheated water instantly flashes to steam.

Inside the boiler, steam forms in the space above the water and is collected at the steam dome, then directed by way of a throttle valve through the dry pipe at the top of the boiler into the cylinders. (In superheated locomotives steam is first re-circulated through the flues using a superheater to raise the working temperature.) Valves incorporated in the cylinder assembly regulate the passage of steam to and from the cylinders. The steam expands and acts upon the pistons, which slide continuously back and forth within the cylinders to transmit reciprocating force to the driving wheels via the rods. After the steam has done its work on the piston, it exits the cylinder through the valves and exhaust passages, and is finally expelled from the engine through the exhaust nozzle and out the smoke stack.

The nozzle/stack arrangement is crucial to efficient operation of the engine. The exhaust creates a draft in the smokebox that draws combustion gases through the firetubes and flues and pulls fresh air into the firebox through grates and other openings. The rate of the exhaust controls and affects the speed of combustion and allows for more complete burning of fuel.

The characteristic "chuff-chuff" sound is caused by steam exiting the exhaust nozzle. For a standard two-cylinder locomotive, chuffs happen at the rate of four chuffs per driver revolution: one stroke forward and one back for each piston.

The exhaust sound is sharpest and most distinct when the locomotive is starting. Forced draft is integral to the efficient operation of the engine. Without effective draft, the fire would smolder in the firebox and fail to produce sufficient steam. The arrangement of the exhaust nozzle contributes to the automatic increase in the exhaust draft as the engine gains speed, which is one of the fundamental attributes of the Stephenson cycle.

Controls

The engineer has two primary controls to regulate the power and speed of the engine. The throttle valve controls the volume of steam going to the cylinders. The reverser (reversing lever) is used to manipulate the valve gear (which synchronizes valve motion). As well as setting the direction of the engine, the reversing lever allows the engineer to regulate the engine speed by adjusting the rate of valve travel, which regulates steam input into the cylinder for a longer or shorter portion of the piston stroke. The act of reducing steam admission allows for faster and more economical operation, which is known as "shortening the cutoff."

"Full cutoff" describes the position of the

Chad Frederickson attends to the linkage on the throttle valve on Reading & Northern 4-6-2 no. 425. Many late-era locomotives had their throttle valves at the front of the locomotive (as this one), rather than the more common position under the steam dome. Placing the throttle valve in the superheater header gave the engineer more precise control by shortening the distance between the throttle valve and cylinders. *Oren B. Helbok*

Santa Fe 2-8-4 no. 4115 is stationary, but it is producing voluminous exhaust because its blower is working to get its fire and boiler up to temperature while being serviced at the Slaton, Texas, engine facility. *Robert A. Witbeck, collection of the Center for Railroad Photography & Art*

Sydney & Louisberg Railway no. 71 receives some maintenance at the Grace Bay, Nova Scotia, roundhouse. The lack of a side rod attached to the drive wheel indicates that this old engine isn't going anywhere on its own. *Jim Shaughnessy, collection of the Center for Railroad Photography & Art*

Arrangement		Name	Typical service
<OO	0-4-0	none	switcher
<OOO	0-6-0	none	switcher
<OOOO	0-8-0	none	switcher
<oOOo	2-4-2	Columbia	freight, passenger
<ooOO	4-4-0	American	freight, passenger
<ooOOo	4-4-2	Atlantic	passenger
<oOOO	2-6-0	Mogul	freight
<oOOOo	2-6-2	Prairie	freight
<ooOOO	4-6-0	Ten-Wheeler	passenger, freight
<ooOOOo	4-6-2	Pacific	passenger
<ooOOOoo	4-6-4	Hudson	passenger
<oOOOO	2-8-0	Consolidation	freight
<oOOOOo	2-8-2	Mikado	freight
<oOOOOoo	2-8-4	Berkshire	fast freight
<ooOOOO	4-8-0	Twelve-Wheeler	freight
<ooOOOOo	4-8-2	Mountain	freight, passenger
<ooOOOOoo	4-8-4	Northern	fast freight, passenger
<oOOOOO	2-10-0	Decapod	freight
<oOOOOOo	2-10-2	Santa Fe	freight
<oOOOOOoo	2-10-4	Texas	fast freight
<ooOOOOOo	4-10-2	Southern Pacific (Overland)	freight, passenger
<ooOOOOOOo	4-12-2	Union Pacific	freight
<OOO OOO	0-6-6-0	Mallet	helper, slow freight
<oOOO OOOo	2-6-6-2	Mallet	freight
<oOOO OOOoo	2-6-6-4	none	freight
<oOOOOOOOOo	2-8-8-2	Mallet	freight
<oOOO OOOooo	2-6-6-6	Allegheny	freight
<oOOOO OOOOoo	2-8-8-4	Yellowstone	freight
<ooOO OOoo	4-4-4-4	Duplex	passenger
<oooOO OOooo	6-4-4-6	Duplex	passenger
<ooOOO OOoo	4-6-4-4	Duplex	freight
<ooOO OOOoo	4-4-6-4	Duplex	freight
<ooOOO OOOoo	4-6-6-4	Challenger	fast freight, passenger
<ooOOOO OOOOoo	4-8-8-4	Big Boy	freight

Wheel arrangements—Whyte classification system

By the 20th century the standard American method of classifying steam locomotives using their wheel arrangements was established as the Whyte System, named for F.M. Whyte. Whyte's logical breakdown of locomotive wheels into their functional groups was indicated by their locations: leading, driving, and trailing, with each group separated by a hyphen. If a locomotive type lacks leading or trailing wheels, a zero is used at these positions.

For example, the common American-type locomotive features a truck with four leading wheels, four driving wheels, and no trailing wheels, so it is classified as a 4-4-0. The Atlantic type, classified as 4-4-2, has a four-wheel leading truck, four driving wheels, and a two-wheel trailing truck.

Articulated and Duplex locomotives, which feature more than one set of drivers, have each driver grouping counted separately. For example, Baltimore & Ohio's pioneer Mallet type with two sets of six driving wheels but no leading or trailing wheels is designated an 0-6-6-0. A Mallet with a two-wheel leading pony truck is a 2-6-6-0, and one with two-wheel leading and trailing trucks is a 2-6-6-2. Specialized tank locomotives carry a "T" suffix (more on those in Chapter 8).

Most standard wheel classifications had names. Some early names were literal, such as the 4-6-0, known as a "Ten-Wheeler." Most names conveyed something about the locomotive or honored the railroad or region that developed or used the wheel arrangement (such as Niagara, Atlantic, and Santa Fe). Other names were common in virtually all regions, including the Mogul (2-6-0), Consolidation (2-8-0), Mikado (2-8-2), and Pacific (4-8-2).

Some names were not universally accepted, such as the 4-8-4. It was a very popular modern wheel arrangement, but was known by a variety of names that depended on the owning railroads. In the Midwest and West they were commonly called Northerns, as they first appeared on the Northern Pacific, but that nickname was not used in the East or South—instead they were known as Dixies (Nashville, Chattanooga & St. Louis), Greenbriers (Chesapeake & Ohio), and Niagaras (New York Central).

Interestingly, many various Mallet compound locomotives were simply called Mallets regardless of the specific wheel arrangements, while simple (single expansion) articulated locomotives tended to receive specific names such the 4-6-6-4 Challenger and the 2-6-6-6 Allegheny.

The Whyte system was limited in its ability to distinguish a variety of important characteristics. It does not indicate locomotive horsepower, tractive effort, weight, intended service, or maximum speeds. Two locomotives may share the same wheel arrangement but otherwise have very little in common. Take for example the 2-6-2 Prairie type, which was introduced as a fast passenger locomotive with tall driving wheels, but later adapted as a nimble slow-speed wheel arrangement for logging and industrial applications.

Often when locomotives were rebuilt their wheel arrangements were altered. In one of the more unusual alterations, Illinois Central rebuilt a 2-8-4 locomotive into 4-6-4. More common was the conversion of old road freight locomotives into switchers by removing leading trucks.

In mountainous territory it was common to double-head steam locomotives to move heavy trains; this was sometimes done on flatlands as well. On July 24, 1948, a Pennsylvania L1s Mikado and J1 2-10-4 work an eastward coal train at AR Tower in Gallitzin, Pa. The train will soon begin its slow descent toward Altoona. *Bruce Fales, Jay Williams collection*

valves set to allow steam to act on the piston throughout nearly the entire piston stroke (traditionally this was roughly 90 percent; on advanced designs some engines limited maximum cutoff to as low as 50 percent). Full cutoff is most advantageous for starting the engine and working hard at very slow speeds when maximum power is required, but it is inefficient and counterproductive once the engine is underway. As the locomotive gains speed, the pistons move back and forth faster, which allows steam less and less time to expand. Exhausting steam before it has fully expanded is not just a waste of energy, but also places back pressure on the piston which retards its progress.

By shortening the cutoff, the engineer limits the steam entering the cylinder, giving steam more space to expand. This conserves energy and water while reducing back-pressure caused by steam exiting the cylinder. The common reversing lever was historically known as a Johnson bar. On more modern engines screw types of reverse were used (although not common in American practice), as well as power reverse equipment using pneumatic controls.

A typical reverser arrangement features neutral in the center position, where no steam is admitted to the cylinders. By moving the reverser past center the valve travel is oriented relative to the movement of the pistons, with one side of center for forward, and the other side for reverse. The farther from center, the longer the rate of steam admission in relation to the stroke.

Once underway, a skillful engineer would choose to regulate the locomotive's power and speed through manipulation of the reverser while only making large adjustments using the throttle. Finesse in this level of control is quite different than the throttle-heavy control typical of internal combustion engines. As the locomotive comes up to the desired speed the engineer gradually shortens the cutoff by bringing the reverser ever closer to the center position.

In the 1930s and 1940s many railroads applied streamlining to steam locomotives for premier passenger service, as above on Chesapeake & Ohio no. 490, an older 4-6-2 being rebuilt to a 4-6-4 in 1946. Beneath modern sheet-metal shrouds, these locomotives were pretty much the same as their common sisters. Maintenance could be complicated by the shrouding. At left, a crew member has folded back part of the cosmetic shrouding atop Southern Pacific 4-8-4 no. 4449 to access the top of the boiler.
Above: Chesapeake & Ohio; Left: Brian Solomon

Union Pacific's 4-8-8-4 Big Boys were modern, powerful, fast coal burners with voracious appetites for fuel and water. They used 14-wheel pedestal-style tenders as shown by no. 4016. This tender holds 28 tons of coal and 24,000 gallons of water. *Robert A. Witbeck, collection of the Center for Railroad Photography & Art*

In a time-honored practice, the fireman on a Pennsylvania I1s Decapod grabs train orders on a hoop from the operator at Leolyn, Pa. on the Elmira Branch. Winter operations could be hazardous to engine crews and operators alike. *Jim Shaughnessy, collection of the Center for Railroad Photography & Art*

This optimizes the use of steam and helps maintain the speed.

Maintaining the fire and keeping the boiler supplied with an adequate volume of water is a continual challenge for the fireman. If the fire isn't hot enough or isn't properly built, the engine will run out of steam. If the fire is too hot the locomotive will produce more steam than is necessary for immediate use. Safety valves are designed to ensure that the prescribed operating boiler pressure isn't exceeded. These are set to lift and release steam when boiler pressure reaches a pre-established threshold. Although safety valves protect the crew and locomotive from the risk of a boiler explosion (a sudden catastrophic event that will destroy the engine and may kill or injure the crew), when the valves lift it represents an undesirable waste of fuel and water.

Maintaining the level of water in the boiler is also crucial to both safe and efficient steam locomotive operation. Overfilling the boiler reduces the area for steam to form, and may result in "water carryover" if water reaches the level of the throttle valve and passes into the cylinders.

With so many moving parts, prober lubrication is vital for steam locomotives. Crew members or other workers checked for hot bearings and journals at every stop, as here on Central Vermont 4-8-2 Mountain no. 601 at White River Junction, Vt., in June 1950. The worker at left is adding oil to a journal box; the worker at right is lubricating rod bearings. *Jim Shaughnessy, collection of the Center for Railroad Photography & Art*

Power and tractive effort

How powerful is a steam locomotive? It can be difficult to determine, because it varies based on so many factors. Total locomotive weight is a general indicator of the overall power and capacity of a locomotive. Weight on drivers is a better indicator of how much it will be able to pull. The two most common measurements cited for steam were tractive effort and, to a lesser extent, horsepower (more specifically, drawbar horsepower). Both are largely theoretical figures when it comes to steam locomotives, but railroads tended to use tractive effort as a good comparison of how much a locomotive can get going, with horsepower showing how fast it can make it go.

Tractive effort is the theoretical force in pounds that a locomotive exerts. The formula for steam locomotives is: Boiler pressure x the square of the cylinder diameter x the piston stroke, all divided by the driver diameter. Even though it's theoretical, it provides a point of comparison among engines. (Tractive effort is not the same as drawbar pull, which is best physically measured by a dynamometer car that can accurately measure the force actually being applied).

Horsepower is another measurement, but it's tough to compare diesels with steam in this regard because they are completely different types

Strasburg Railroad no. 475, a former Norfolk & Western 4-8-0, approaches East Strasburg, Pa., on a cool evening in November 2008. This popular tourist railroad maintains classic steam traditions by operating a variety of historic locomotives for the benefit of the public. *Brian Solomon*

of machines. Baldwin developed a complex formula for calculating steam locomotive horsepower across a range of speeds based on many additional factors, including boiler pressure, evaporative surface area, piston surface area, temperature of superheated steam, and other variables. The formula was widely used by railroads and other manufacturers, and provides a curve across speeds (horsepower increases as speed increases). A dynamometer car on a train can give a good reading of drawbar horsepower, but only for that particular weight in that situation—a steam locomotive won't put out more horsepower than is required for a given situation, so a maximum load would be required to measure a locomotive's top horsepower.

Railroad mechanical gurus (designers and engineers) used many designs, wheel arrangements, driver diameters, and weights (not to mention other variables) to get what they needed from a particular locomotive. The ultimate design came down to this: how much weight do you need to pull, and how fast do you want to pull it? Ancillary questions included: what are your ruling grades, and what are your track, bridge, weight, and clearance limits and restrictions?

The end result is a tremendous variety of steam locomotives built over the years, many of which—even though designs varied widely—apparently accomplished the same basic task but in wildly disperate ways.

The smokebox door is open on Southern Pacific semi-streamlined class GS-4 4-8-4 no. 4453. The view reveals the exhaust nozzles and pipes that direct exhaust steam from the cylinders upward through the stack. *Southern Pacific*

This greatly reduces steam power, wastes energy, and can cause cylinder damage: Because water cannot be compressed, if it collects in the cylinder, serious damage to the cylinder heads and pistons may result. In extreme circumstances this can result in a blown cylinder head or bent crosshead or main rod. Cylinder drain cocks can be opened when starting the engine in order to purge accumulated water and avoid damage.

More dangerous is low boiler water. If the level of boiler water drops too low, it will fail to cover the top of the firebox (known as the crown sheet). Without water covering it, the extreme heat of the firebox will weaken the metal and lead to failure of the crown sheet, which can result in a boiler explosion.

Among the safety devices on a locomotive are sight glasses to monitor the water level (installed in the cab on the boiler's backhead). These vertical tubes show the actual top level of boiler water with the glass low point positioned above the top of the crown sheet. Many modern steam locomotives featured low-water alarms and fusible plugs that are designed to melt and release steam to avoid a complete crown sheet failure.

A danger is that impure water can result in mineral buildup that clogs the water glasses and produces a false high reading—an inaccurate measure of the amount of water in boiler. To avoid this, the glasses must be "blown down" on a regular basis by directing pressurized water through the glass to eliminate mineral buildup and ensure a free flow of water.

The next chapter takes a more detailed look at boiler and firebox details and design, and how the various types of fuel (wood, coal, and oil) affect steam locomotive design and operation.

The last steam locomotive built for a Class 1 railroad was Norfolk & Western 0-8-0 no. 244, built by the railroad in 1953. It posed for a builder's photo at Shaffers Crossing in Roanoke, Va., in 1953. *Norfolk & Western*

The frame, boiler, and associated components of a Union Pacific 4-8-2 have been lifted off the running gear with a crane during overhaul. This underside view provides a clear illustration of the locomotive frame. *Union Pacific*

4205

Chapter 2

Boiler and firebox design and accessories

Canadian National Railways 2-10-2 no. 4205 is at Montreal in June 1946. It was built in 1919 for Boston & Albany and was sold to CNR after B&A bought its Super Power Class A1 Berkshires in the mid-1920s. The CNR added an Elesco feedwater heater, the laterally mounted cylinder atop the smokebox. Feedwater heaters were among the many devices that improved boiler efficiency in the early 1900s. *G.W. Parks photo, Robert A. Buck collection*

The boiler and firebox are the heart and lungs of a locomotive. Using fuel efficiently and making steam efficiently—and making it fast enough to satisfy the needs of the locomotive—are key factors in locomotive design. Ancillary components such as stokers, injectors, feedwater heaters, and superheaters were all developed to evaporate more water and do it faster, leading to increased power and speed.

Wood as fuel

In the steam locomotive's formative years, wood was the dominant fuel. The abundant timber stands in the eastern United States, where rail lines were spreading rapidly, meant wood was cheap and plentiful. Although early in locomotive development some railroads dabbled with anthracite (hard coal), in general wood remained the preferred fuel until after the Civil War.

Wood-burning locomotives had several distinctive design characteristics. One of the properties of a wood fire is a propensity to generate airborne sparks and burning embers. Since these can cause fires and damage equipment, line-side structures, and freight—as well as possibly injure passengers and employees—railroads sought means to keep sparks from spreading. The most obvious way of minimizing the danger was to prevent embers' exit from the locomotive in the first place. Locomotive builders devised a variety of elaborate smokestacks aimed at containing sparks and embers, and these tall stacks became emblematic of the mid-19th century locomotive.

Most stacks contained internal screens or other methods of filtration. Complicating the smokestack design was that to function efficiently it couldn't interfere with firebox draft or risk limiting the engine's performance. Popular designs included the "bonnet stack" (or "balloon stack") that employed a conical matrix and screens to trap sparks, while not restricting exiting exhaust gases. A balloon stack resembled a large inverted cone. They were a common feature on classic wood-burning engines. Noted for their popularity on lines in the West, bonnet stacks were in fact employed by railroads across the continent.

Coal takes over

The rise of coal as a locomotive fuel went hand in hand with rapid railroad expansion in the decades following the Civil War. As

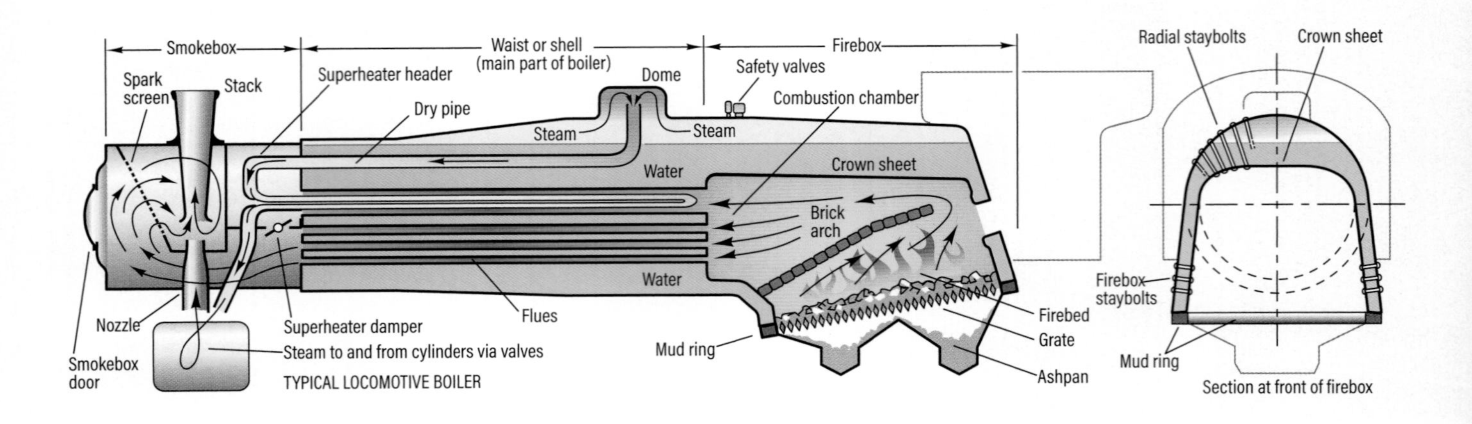

TYPICAL LOCOMOTIVE BOILER

Locomotive *York*, no. 17, is a faithfully re-created replica of a mid-19th century Rogers wood-burning 4-4-0. It features a classic headlight, colorfully decorated pilot, drive-wheel centers, and sand dome, with a hardwood cab and conical "bonnet"-style smokestack designed to filter hot embers.
Adam Stuebgen

railroads expanded operations and territory, they served as the engine for industrial growth and helped open up bituminous coal fields in western Pennsylvania, western Maryland, central Appalachia, and southern Illinois. Soft bituminous coal was both cheaper to mine and easier to burn than anthracite (hard) coal, and was well suited as locomotive fuel. The growing abundance of bituminous coal drove its price down and this, combined with a rising cost of timber, the depletion of many forest areas, and expansive railroad growth, accelerated the shift away from wood as the primary locomotive fuel.

Coal-hauling lines made the conversion to coal first, but by the last two decades of the century most other railroads had made the switch as well, and by the 1890s roughly 90 percent of American railroads were using coal-burning locomotives. Coal-fired engines necessitated specialized boiler and firebox design, and these altered overall performance and appearance. Coal produced fewer sparks but more soot and smoke, and the drafting requirements for coal were different. Locomotives no longer needed elaborate stacks to filter hot sparks, but the exhaust was significantly dirtier. Increased soot and grime contributed to railroads abandoning the elaborately styled and colorfully painted engines characteristic of the wood-burning era. In general, coal-fired locomotives took on a somber spartan appearance as all-black steam locomotives with minimal adornment emerged as the new standard in the late 1800s.

The switch to coal had profound and lasting changes for railroad operations. Coal has a higher burn (heat) value than wood, which enabled a single fireman to handle more fuel and contributed to a rapid growth in locomotive size and power. Coaling towers were erected at locomotive facilities

Bituminous coal is the preferred fuel for steam locomotives. On a typical run, a firemen will shovel several tons of it from the tender into the firebox. It must be clean, free of debris, and properly sized (lumps under 4") to burn well in the firebox. *Brian Solomon*

and strategic lineside locations to allow for rapid refueling of engines, making it a much faster process than filling a tender with wood.

The conversion to coal coincided with a variety of changes to firebox design, some of which anticipated the change to coal but others mandated to accommodate coal burning. In his book *A History of the American Locomotive,* John H. White Jr., suggests that some firebox alterations were largely ineffective and unnecessary, and it turned out that only a few minor modifications to the basic wood-burning firebox design of the period were actually suited for bituminous coal. Other changes were crucial to successful coal firing. In the wood-burning era copper had served as a primary material in firebox construction owing to the durability of this material. However, bituminous coal combustion produced destructive acids that resulted in rapid deterioration of copper surfaces, which led to the widespread shift to wrought iron for firebox construction and the related heating surfaces.

Another significant addition was the firebrick arch. This is a partition inside the firebox chamber constructed from an angled row of bricks mounted on arch tubes between the grates and the fire tubes. This forced combustion gases to take a less direct path to the fire tubes, making fuel consumption more efficient and resulting in cleaner burning of fuel.

Until 1900, all locomotives were hand-fired—the fireman hand-shoveled coal from the tender into the firebox. Manual (hand-operated) firebox doors gave way to pneumatic, foot-powered pedals that allow hands-free operation of the firebox door. In the early 1900s, as locomotive size began rapidly increasing, firemen could no longer keep up with the demands of the engine. A single fireman could shovel about 2 to 2½ tons of coal an hour; new locomotives in the early 1900s could burn 3 to 4 tons an hour, and modern articulateds of the late steam era could go through 11 tons an hour.

Railroads' initial solution was to add another fireman. It was cumbersome, as there's only so much room in a locomotive cab, and railroads didn't like paying an extra employee. It did, however, work, and some railroads continued doing this (especially on fast passenger runs or on runs going up heavy grades).

The eventual solution became the stoker, a mechanical device that carried coal from the tender to the firebox. Several methods were tried, including conveyor belts and belts with paddles or small buckets. The eventual solution was auger-style (screw-type) conveyors in tubes.

The lower inside walls of the tender sloped toward a longitudinal slot at bottom, where the conveyor was open. This conveyor carried coal through a connection with the locomotive under the cab deck. One or two vertical augers then elevated the coal upward into the firebox.

To keep incoming coal from simply being dumped into the firebox, a series of steam jets then blew the coal different directions to evenly distribute it throughout the firebox. The fireman controlled each of these jets with valves; he also controlled operations of the stoker itself.

The largest manufacturer of these devices was the Standard Stoker Co. It offered the Type A (Duplex) version, which had two vertical augers to distribute coal to both sides of the firebox; and the Type B, which used a single elevating screw. Other manufacturers offered stokers that operated in similar manner.

Even with a stoker, the fireman remained busy making sure the fire was burning properly. The feed had to be regulated constantly depending upon how the engine was being used, especially if speed varied widely or the train was going up and down hills. In many ways, the job could be more challenging: because so much coal was being burned so quickly, situations could escalate in a hurry if problems weren't noticed right away.

(And if you ever want to raise the ire of a former steam fireman, refer to a stoker as "automatic"—you'll undoubtedly hear something to the effect of "There wasn't anything automatic about 'em!" with a few other choice words thrown in.)

Even with the advent of stokers, some railroads were reluctant to invest in them because of cost. Regulations eventually required stokers on any passenger engine weighing more than 160,000 pounds on drivers (175,000 pounds for freight locomotives). Many smaller locomotives—namely switchers and many older locomotives that remained in branch-line or secondary service—remained hand-fired until the end of the steam era.

Firebox design

The firebox is at the rear (cab end) of the boiler, placed in the boiler so that its top

A Burlington Route 4-8-4 takes on coal and water. Maintaining coaling stations and water towers was a large expense for railroads, and steam locomotives had to stop frequently to replenish both. *Robert Hundman*

Stoker-equipped locomotives have tenders with openings at the bottom, which allowed coal to enter the screw-type auger. Behind the sloped walls is the water tank, which wraps around the coal bunker. This is a Union Pacific Big Boy tender. *Jim Wrinn*

and sides are covered by water. The gap, or spacing, between the firebox walls and top (crown sheet) is maintained by hundreds of staybolts that pass from the firebox surface through the gap to the boiler cover. The boiler is covered by insulation (usually asbestos-based) and metal jacketing, so the heads of the staybolts aren't visible unless you're seeing a locomotive under construction or repair.

Through the 1890s, fireboxes—like locomotives—were small, with only 15 square feet or so of grate area (the bottom surface that holds the burning coal). These fireboxes were narrow, to fit between the driving wheels. As locomotives got bigger, the firebox became wider—at first riding atop the drivers, then placed behind them, supported by trailing-truck wheels. Their profiles generally blended with the boiler profile.

A couple of distinctive variations were used on some locomotives. The Belpaire firebox was wider at the top, with a squared profile that protruded from the round boiler profile. Its key advantage was providing a larger evaporative surface and better heat transfer compared to a standard rounded-top firebox. It was also more expensive to produce. The main users of Belpaire fireboxes were the Great Northern and Pennsylvania railroads.

The other significant design was the Wooten firebox, designed specifically to burn anthracite. In the early years of U.S. railroads, the Philadelphia & Reading emerged as America's leading anthracite hauler. Despite this, the railroad found that using anthracite (also known as "hard coal," as it is rock-like) as locomotive fuel was problematic owing to the difficulty of getting it to burn initially, and then making use of the great intensity of the heat produced once it finally ignited. Since Reading had ample amounts of anthracite waste ("culm") available for very low cost, it was interested in finding ways to use it as fuel. Culm, although having waste rock blended with the anthracite, still had a lot of heat value in it—but the challenges of burning anthracite were further exacerbated.

In 1877, P&R's general manager, John E. Wootten, addressed the problem of burning anthracite culm by inventing a shallow and unusually wide firebox to provide adequate grate area to facilitate ignition and complete combustion of the slow-burning material. What became known as the Wootten firebox provided 2.5 times more grate area than the typical steam locomotive firebox of the period, making it too big to be located within the locomotive frame as was typical of contemporary fireboxes.

Instead, Wootten placed the firebox above the locomotive frame, riding over the rear driving wheels, with the base of the firebox the full width of the locomotive. This didn't allow sufficient room at the rear of the locomotive for a full standard cab, so a separate engineer's cab was built straddling the boiler ahead of the firebox, while the fireman rode behind the firebox

The front end of this tender shows the end of the stoker's auger conveyor, which will align with a similar connection on the locomotive when coupled. *Trains magazine collection*

The round opening just below the deck of this Santa Fe 2-8-4 is the auger connection for the stoker, which mates with the connection on the tender. This is a Duplex stoker; note the two vertical conveyor columns above the cab deck, with "KEEP HANDS OUT" lettering on the removable access plates. *Baldwin*

on a narrow platform. This awkward split-cab locomotive became known as a "Camelback" or "Mother Hubbard."

They were widely built from the 1880s into the 1910s for a variety of railroads, most of them anthracite haulers, and employing a great variety of wheel arrangements from Reading's compact 0-4-0 switchers to ungainly 4-6-2 Pacifics, along with massive Alco-built 0-8-8-0 Mallet compounds for the Erie Railroad. Other railroads operating large numbers of Camelbacks included Central of New Jersey; Delaware & Hudson; Delaware, Lackawanna & Western; Lehigh & Hudson River; Lehigh & New England; Lehigh Valley; and New York, Ontario & Western.

The design fell out of favor for safety and convenience issues; also, new, more powerful locomotives were being built with large, wide fireboxes carried behind the drivers (supported by trailing trucks), offering better solutions than the split-cab Camelback design (contrary to rumor, the Interstate Commerce Commission never issued a formal ban on the design). Few were built after the mid-1910s and none after 1927, but many remained in operation through the 1940s.

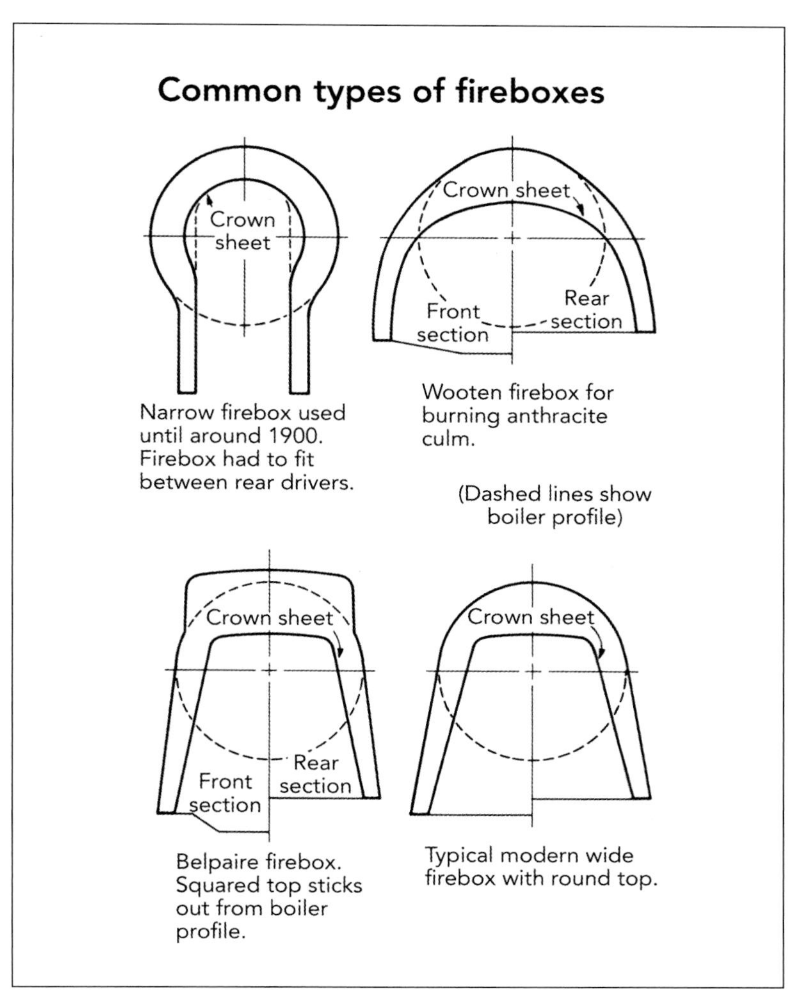

Firebox designs evolved from the mid-1800s onward. The drawings show cross-sections of the early (narrow) fire-box, Wooten (early wide) firebox, Belpaire firebox, and the modern firebox. *Kalmbach Media*

Oil-fired locomotives

Railroads in the East and Midwest were blessed with ample access to coal, but railroads in the West and Southwest faced a dearth of this common fuel. Not only did these railroads have no on-line coal mines—coal had to be shipped long distances, making the fuel far more expensive to acquire.

By the 1890s, large oil deposits had been discovered in Oklahoma, Texas, and California, and the petroleum industry was growing as internal-combustion vehicles were quickly becoming more common. Baldwin built a test locomotive in 1894 (a Vauclain compound 4-6-0) to burn oil, based on a design that had been successfully used in Russia; it did well enough to encourage further development.

Around that time, the Santa Fe and Southern Pacific were both seeking to make use of locally produced petroleum for locomotive fuel on lines in Southern California. The Santa Fe teamed with the Union Oil Company and developed a device for distributing oil into a locomotive firebox to enable adequate combustion. By the turn of the 20th century, Santa Fe and Southern Pacific were both using oil-fired locomotives, and other Western railroads followed, including Union Pacific and Western Pacific.

Oil offered several advantages over coal. It had a higher heat value (per pound) than

The Pennsylvania Railroad was one of a few U.S. railroads to commonly use the Belpaire firebox, apparent for its boxy profile extending above the boiler outline (in front of the cab). Here PRR K4s 5377 simmers at East St. Louis, Ill., on October, 28 1944. *R.A. Frederick collection*

Camelback locomotives feature wide ("Wooten") fireboxes for burning anthracite culm. They required moving the engineer's cab forward astride the boiler, with a small platform at the rear for the fireman. Lehigh & New England no. 122, an 0-8-0, is among the last Camelbacks built (in 1927 by Baldwin). *Baldwin*

coal. It left no ashes or firebox residue, which allowed locomotives to travel farther (since there was no ash pan to require regular dumping). Burning cinders did not escape the stack. It was also easier to handle than coal. Many railroads in other regions also moved to oil, often for passenger service or in regions where coal was expensive to obtain or where sparks could easily cause lineside fires.

The fuel used was typically heavy oil, then commonly known as Bunker C (in later-day terms, No. 6 fuel oil). Bunker C's main appeal is that it was inexpensive, as it was largely the residual that remained after lighter fuels had been refined from it (kerosene, gasoline, and lighter oils). Because of its thick viscosity, it required heating to flow. Steam lines were routed into the tender, which heated it prior to being pumped to the firebox. The tender tank on some locomotives was pressurized (typically at 5 psi) to aid with flow.

Oil firing required significant firebox alterations including changes to firebox grates, firebox doors, and the way the engine was drafted. In the firebox, steam was used to atomize the oil under pressure at the burners. Larger combustion chambers were also used, which conserved the heat better and resulted in more efficient boiler operation. The fireman controlled the rate of burn and oil flow with a valve. Depending on its size and power (and how hard it was being worked), a locomotive could burn 6 to 12 gallons of oil per mile.

Downsides included faster firebox erosion, which could lead to higher maintenance costs. The smoke and soot from oil burning could quickly line the flues, resulting in poor combustion and poor heat transfer with boiler water. The solution for this was for the fireman to toss a couple shovelfuls of sand into the firebox when the locomotive was working hard. Called "sanding the flues," the strong draft pulled

A worker is welding at the boiler end of a firebox of a Norfolk & Western locomotive at the railroad's Roanoke Shops in the 1950s. The flues and flue sheet are visible behind the worker; the pipes in the foreground are circulators from the boiler. *Robert Hale*

Staybolts hold the firebox in position with proper spacing between it and the boiler exterior. Here we're looking from the boiler back into the firebox (with the flues and tube sheets removed) as a worker uses a torch to cut a staybolt during restoration of Union Pacific Big Boy no. 4014. *Jim Wrinn*

3777

the sand in through the inspection opening and through the flues, scouring them and removing the soot. Since the process produced thick black clouds of smoke, when possible crews sanded flues when out of public view.

Spotting an oil-fired locomotive is usually a matter of looking at the tender—there's no exposed coal bunker. Tenders for oil burners are generally boxy and rectangular, with two rooftop hatches—one for oil at the front and water toward the rear. Oil tenders are often larger than comparable coal tenders to allow a longer range between topping off water and fuel.

Locomotives could be converted from coal to oil, and there are numerous examples of locomotives built as oil-burners being converted to coal, and back again, as best suited railroad operations based on fuel availability and cost.

Water and boilers

Water seems like it would be a simple thing to deal with, but ensuring a reliable water supply and then getting it into the boiler could be a challenge. A hard-working locomotive rapidly consumes steam, so boiler water needs regular replenishment of feedwater. We're talking a *lot* of water: Many modern steam locomotives could evaporate 10,000 gallons of water or more in

Oil-burning Santa Fe 4-8-4 no. 3777 was built by Baldwin in 1941. Oil enabled longer runs because there was no need to dump ashes from the firebox. To allow some locomotives to travel even farther between fuel and water stops, Santa Fe equipped some of its oil burners with extremely large tenders. This one has a capacity of 25,000 gallons of water and 7,000 gallons of fuel oil; eight-wheel trucks help distribute the greater weight. *Robert A. Witbeck, collection of the Center for Railroad Photography & Art*

The front of this oil tender (the end facing the locomotive cab) includes a temperature gauge (at right), next to a valve that regulates the steam line that heats the oil. The **DANGER** sign warns against having open flames near the tender. *TRAINS magazine collection*

Fireboxes on oil-fired engines have a small inspection opening that's much smaller than the firebox door opening on a coal locomotive. Here Ed Dickens checks the fire on Union Pacific Big Boy no. 4014 during a 2019 trip following its restoration. *John Crisanti*

an hour; large locomotives and articulated engines even more.

Engine crews were more concerned with having an adequate water supply than with having enough fuel—quite simply, because their lives literally depended upon it. Not only does the boiler require ample water to continue its production of steam—it's critical to maintain enough water in the boiler to keep the top of the firebox (the crown sheet) submerged. If the boiler water level drops and the crown sheet is no longer covered, the extreme heat of the firebox will weaken the metal of the crown sheet until it fails. When this hot metal under high pressure gives way, the superheated water in the boiler flashes to steam, with a boiler explosion the result: a catastrophic event that usually destroyed the locomotive and killed its crew. As a result, enginemen developed a healthy concern for regularly inspecting and maintaining proper boiler water level.

Ensuring a proper water supply could be a challenge. Railroads used wells, lakes, rivers, and other sources to keep their lineside water tanks supplied. One issue was that water varied in quality by region. Some water contains a lot of minerals and other impurities. This can result in foaming while boiling, and in leaving deposits behind in the boiler after the water evaporates. If you've ever cleaned out an old pot or pan you know how bad this scale and gunk can be—now picture the same thing in a boiler that holds several thousand gallons. Scale lining the inside of the boiler along the flues and firebox surfaces inhibits proper heat transfer and cuts down the boiler's efficiency.

Railroads fought this in several ways. Among the most common was chemical

SANTA FE
3437

A Santa Fe hostler fills a tender with oil from a standpipe by positioning the pipe and then turning a long extension to the on/off valve. The standpipe is connected to a trackside tank (out of sight) by underground piping. The locomotive is 4-6-2 no. 3437; its tender has a capacity of 8,000 gallons of oil and 20,000 gallons of water. *Santa Fe*

pellets or cakes that crew members were supposed to add to the tender each time it was filled. Some railroads built treatment plants at key locations to provide better water.

Simply having water at all was an issue in some areas, particularly in the desert Southwest. The Santa Fe and Southern Pacific both had to have large fleets of tank cars for water service, which were carried in solid trains to supply water tanks along these routes. The lack of water more than any other factor led to the early dieselization of these routes starting in the early 1940s.

Feedwater pumps and steam injectors

A challenge in early steam locomotive design was the difficulty in reliably re-supplying feedwater to the boiler once the engine was up to pressure and on the move. The difficulty was that water had to be forced into the boiler at a higher pressure than the boiler pressure itself, a difficult task for a standard pump.

Early locomotives were equipped with feedwater pumps. Among the most common varieties were crosshead-powered pumps and those driven by eccentrics or return cranks. John White Jr. wrote that these early pumps suffered from frequent operational failures and were a chronic source of complaints from engine crews. It's not difficult to imagine the fear and frustration of a crew, who when facing low boiler water had to fight with a cantankerous pump acting up at precisely the wrong moment.

Among the fundamental problems faced by most 1800s-era feedwater pumps was that the engine needed to be moving for the pump to work—and if the engine was laboring, it was not moving fast enough to supply water as quickly as the boiler required it. This resulted in situations where the engine was effectively starving itself of water as it worked harder. Pumps could also freeze in the winter, increasing the risk

Union Pacific 4-8-4 no. 822 double-heads with another 4-8-4 on eastbound train 24, the *Pacific Limited*. These locomotives were built in 1939 to burn coal; they are shown here after their conversion to oil burners in 1946. They were retired in the late 1950s. *Robert A. Witbeck, collection of the Center for Railroad Photography & Art*

of boiler explosions when the temperature dropped.

An innovation and alternative to the feedwater pump was the steam injector. Developed in the mid-19th century, the injector began to make a limited appearance on American locomotives beginning in 1860. This ingenious innovation used a high-velocity steam jet to force water into the boiler under pressure, and also offered a secondary advantage of preheating boiler water and thus minimizing the drop in boiler pressure that occurred when cold water was introduced to an active boiler.

The typical steam injector was a comparatively simple device without mechanical moving parts. The most common type used live steam (steam produced by the boiler), although a later innovation was the development of an exhaust steam injector. The injector had intake inlets, sometimes called receiving tubes, for feedwater delivery; live steam from the boiler was forced through a combining tube featuring a conical nozzle (which increased its pressure). The result was a high-pressure jet that propelled steam-heated water via a delivery pipe past a check valve and into the boiler. Drain cocks and overflow pipes were designed for situations when excessive feedwater entered the injector.

In his 1874 book *Catechism of the Locomotive,* Matthias Forney offered this description of injector operation: "Steam escaping from under pressure has a much higher velocity than water would have under the same pressure and condition. The escaping steam from the receiving tube unites with the feed water in the combining tube, and gives to this water a velocity greater than it would have if escaping directly from the water-space in the boiler. The power of this water to enter the boiler comes from its weight moving at the velocity acquired from the steam, and it is thus enabled to overcome the boiler pressure."

However, despite their simple construction, early injectors were comparatively frail. They were difficult to operate and were also unpopular with locomotive crews. Among their common problems was that as they delivered hot boiler water they absorbed heat; the hotter they became, the less effective they were in water delivery. If they became too hot, they sometimes ceased working altogether.

Boiler components are quite visible in this 1930 under-construction view of a Chesapeake & Ohio 2-10-4: Large firebox at left, mounted behind and below the drivers, supported by a four-wheel trailing truck; high-capacity boiler; and smokebox (right). Modern "Super-Power" steam locomotives were designed with high boiler capacity to haul heavy trains at high speeds. *Lima-Hamilton*

Water was critical to operation, but more importantly to the crew, keeping sufficient water in the boiler was a matter of safety. Here a fireman tops off the tank on a Baltimore & Ohio Chicago Terminal switcher in 1956. *Jim Shaughnessy*

Despite their early problems, gradual improvements to injector design, combined with a better understanding of how to use the equipment, effectively resulted in near-universal application of injectors to locomotives by the end of the 1800s. Injectors would remain standard equipment on most locomotives until the end of the steam era. Each locomotive had two sources of boiler water. This could be an injector on each side, or an injector on one side and a feedwater heater on the other.

Injectors are of two types: lifting and non-lifting. A lifting injector can draw water up the feed pipe from a lower level. A non-lifting injector requires that water be fed to it by gravity, meaning it's always mounted low on a locomotive (below the floor of the tender tank)—usually on the right side under the cab. Lifting injectors are usually located alongside the boiler in front of the cab on the left side of the locomotive.

Feedwater heaters

A challenge in boiler efficiency is that its feedwater, coming from the tender, is significantly cooler than the water that's already in the boiler. When cool water is added to the boiler, pressure falls and significant additional heat is required to bring the water back to operating temperature. Finding a way to increase the temperature of the feedwater thus greatly improves the efficiency of the boiler.

BALDWIN LOCOMOTIVE WORKS
28
PHILADELPHIA U.S.A.

Keeping the boiler clean and free of sediment is vital to efficiency. Here the crew of Sierra Railway no. 28 blows down the boiler, opening lower blow-down valves and using steam pressure to expel steam and water to flush out accumulated mineral deposits. Baldwin built the 2-8-0 in 1922; it still operates in excursion service. *Brian Solomon*

Feedwater heaters do exactly that. They conserve energy by recycling exhaust steam (which otherwise would be wasted) to preheat water pumped from the tender prior to admission into the boiler. The hotter the water admitted to the boiler, the less additional heat it required to boil; the result was a more-efficient locomotive.

In the early 1900s, various locomotive component supply firms began marketing boiler feedwater heaters as an alternative to the common steam injector. After World War I, feedwater heaters emerged as standard equipment on many late-era locomotive designs, and were added as an upgrade to some older engines.

The two principle varieties of feedwater heater are the closed and open types. Both enjoyed commercial success by presenting notable commercial advantages. In the 1938 edition of the *Locomotive Cyclopedia,* The Superheater Company explained the main advantage of feedwater heaters: "For each 11-degree rise in the temperature of the feedwater fed into the boiler, there is a savings of approximately one per cent of the fuel burned."

The open-type feedwater heater is characterized by a pump heating system where exhaust steam comes in direct contact with feedwater. This system mandates the use of an oil separator to prevent cylinder lubrication oils being carried through the exhaust from contaminating boiler water. However, the open system benefits from an uninterrupted water circuit, and may be delivered by either a high-speed centrifugal-type pump or a common slow-speed reciprocating pump. The Worthington Pump and Machinery Corporation was a primary supplier of the open type.

By the 1930s, Worthington offered two basic open feedwater heater designs. Its SA system used three separate components that were located in different places on the locomotive. A 1938 advertisement details

The fireman on Union Pacific Challenger no. 3985 carefully watches the injector and sight glass as the boiler fills with water. Maintaining the proper water level in the boiler is vital to both efficient boiler operation and safety. *Tom Kline*

this equipment: "The Type SA Locomotive Feedwater Heating Equipment consists of . . . the cold water pump, the heater, and the hot water pump. These units are small and therefore permit considerable flexibility of application to secure the most desirable arrangement with the space limitations. This type of feedwater heater is particularly well adapted to meet the application requirements of modern locomotives. In general, the cold water pump is applied under the cab, the heater is applied in the smokebox either in front of or behind the stack, and the hot water pump is located either on the front of the locomotive or well forward on the side of the boiler under the running board. The equipment is controlled by a single steam valve located inside the cab."

Because the components of this system were smaller and located in different places on the locomotive, the Type SA feedwater heater is less obvious than common types of large single-unit heaters, such as the Elesco. The equipment was designed, as described in Worthington's 1938 ad, so that "cold water from the tender is supplied to the heater by a variable-speed turbine-driven low-pressure centrifugal cold water pump. The cold water is delivered through the heater cover into a spray chamber where it mixes with exhaust steam. This exhaust steam from the locomotive passes into the heater from the bottom through exhaust check valves. After the water is heated, it flows down through the hot water outlet into the hot water pump which delivers it to the boiler. The water level in the heater is controlled by the float-actuated control valve. This valve regulates the amount of steam to the cold water turbine."

Worthington's Type BL-2 Feedwater Heater was a single unit, whereby both cold and hot water pumps and heater were combined in a self-contained machine. The basic operation was similar to the type

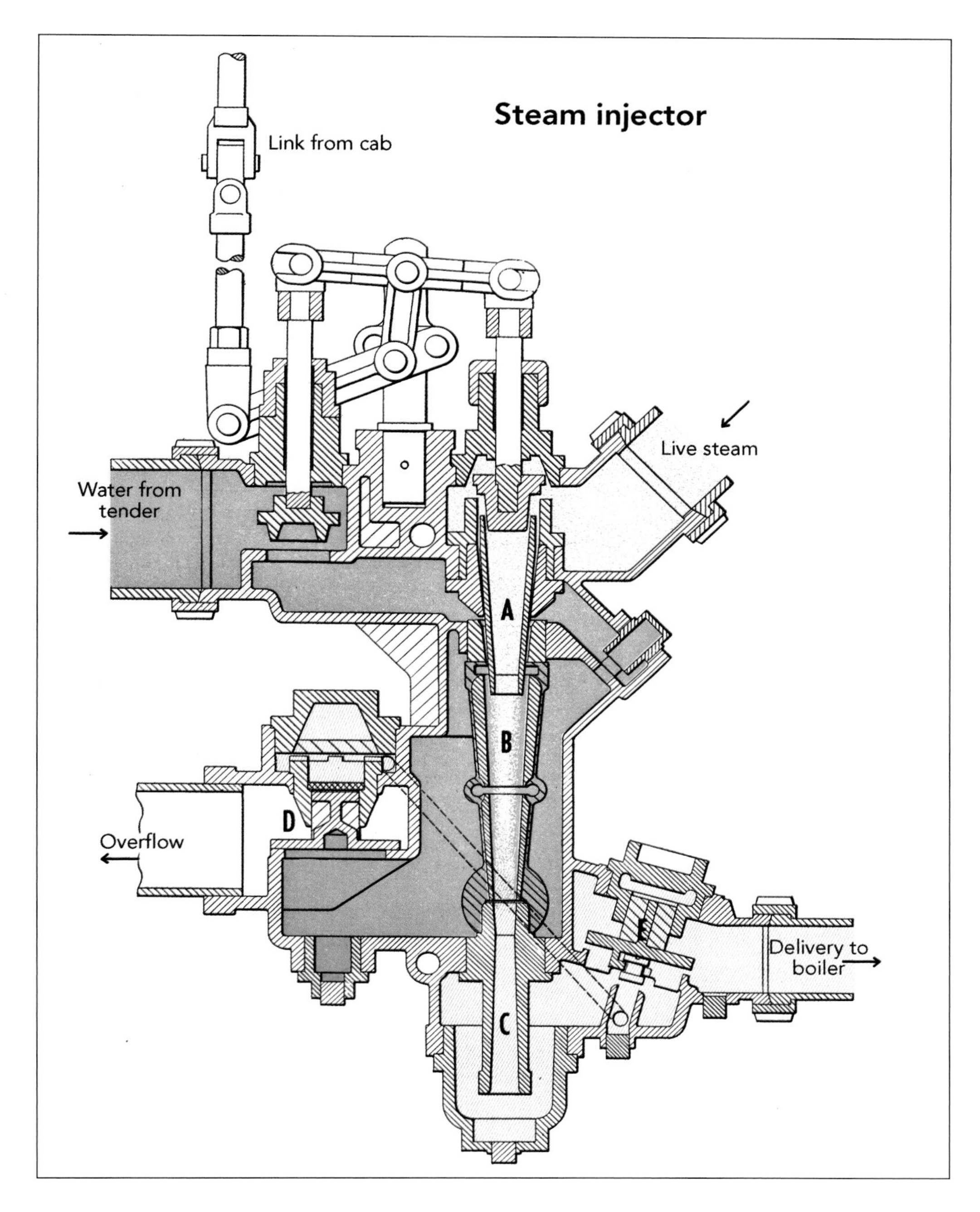

An injector works by combining steam (from the boiler) with incoming water from the tender. Forcing the steam through conical nozzles increases the pressure, allowing the water to be forced into the boiler through a check valve (at the boiler entrance). *Trains magazine collection*

SA, but with the BL-2 both pumps were operated by the same piston rod. A different valve arrangement controlled the water and steam levels. Worthington boasted that both of its feedwater heating systems provided open heating systems that were unaffected by scale accumulation and offered high feedwater temperatures to afford significant fuel savings. These feedwater supply systems also conserved water and required less-frequent boiler maintenance, while enabling increased drawbar pulling power, which meant that engines so equipped were both more efficient and more powerful.

Closed-system feedwater heaters employed separate circuits that directed water through networks of tubes immersed in exhaust steam. These systems prevented exhaust from directly contacting feedwater, so in theory eliminated the need for an oil

Non-lifting injectors must be located below the level of the water supply—in this case under the cab on the right side of Milwaukee Road 4-6-2 no. 812.
Milwaukee Road

separator for the boiler feed, while helping to conserve water. Closed-type feedwater heaters were manufactured by the J.S. Coffin, Jr., Co. of Englewood, N.J., and the Superheater Company of New York, which sold the easily recognizable cylindrical Elesco heater.

In the 1922 *Locomotive Cyclopedia,* the Superheater Company offered this detailed explanation of the Elesco feedwater heater: "The complete apparatus consists of a boiler feed pump, a heater, a filter, and the necessary piping. The feedwater passes from the tender tank through the suction line to the pump which forces it through the heater and into the boiler. Exhaust steam is piped from the valve chambers and the air and water pumps to the heater where its heat is imparted to the feedwater. The condensate formed is passed through a filter to remove the oil and then it goes to the tender for use again."

Since the Elesco design aimed to maximize the conservation of locomotive water, even though exhaust steam didn't directly contact boiler water, a filter was still used because water was returned to the tender rather than expelled from the locomotive. The tube arrangement inside the heater was engineered to facilitate the greatest degree of heat transfer from exhaust to feedwater, while minimizing the resistance of water flowing through the heating unit. The 1922 article details types of Elesco heaters. For example, the heater used on a large locomotive would have "about 180 copper tubes, ⅝" outside diameter and 1⁄16" inch thick, the ends of which are secured by being rolled into grooves in two heavy tube plates in such a manner as to prevent leakage effectively. The resulting nest of tubes is enclosed within a cast-iron cylinder and end casings. At one end of the heater the tube plate is bolted to the flange of the body. The other tube plate is not rigidly fastened to the body but fits inside and bears in such a way as to slide back and forth with contraction and expansion of the tubes. Bolted to each tube sheet is a cast-steel header with partitions so arranged that the end of the tubes are divided into four groups and the water is thus compelled to travel the length of the heater four times, absorbing heat as it goes."

Operation of the Elesco unit was fairly straightforward, but required an understanding of its workings to make optimum use of it: "Before starting the pump, the engineman should see that the valves in the exhaust lines to the heater, the boiler check valve, and the tank valve are [all] open. The drain at the heater and those on the pump should be closed. The lubricator should be opened to feed about one drop per minute and the steam valve slightly cracked to clear the pump of water and insure its operation. Thereafter no further attention is necessary other than operating the steam valve to control the pump speed. The pump should be operated as little as possible when the locomotive valve is closed as the heat can effect no saving when no exhaust steam is available. There is no objection to using the pump for short periods while the locomotive is not working steam since the exhaust from the air pumps, headlight turbine, and water pump are discharged into the heater and will heat the feed water to a fairly high temperature and prevent damage to the boiler from cold water."

The Coffin feedwater heater is identifiable as a large inverted U-shaped appliance matching the diameter of the locomotive boiler. On some locomotives this was neatly concealed in the smokebox, often immediately ahead of the exhaust stack. On other engines, a lack of available space resulted in the Coffin heater being mounted on top of or in front of the smokebox, giving a locomotive an awkward front-heavy appearance. In 1938, Coffin offered five variations of this heater, differing primarily by capacity. Coffin's advertisement in the 1938 *Locomotive Cyclopedia* describes its closed system as a "curved tube bundle containing five high-velocity tube passages through which the water flows in turbulent manner without the use of agitators in the tubes. Each tube is definitely locked at four points. Tube sheets are copper faced. The heads are bronze. There are no moving parts."

It goes on to explain the working of the heater: "Exhaust steam from the cylinders enters the steam passage at the rear of the compartment and flows, in the counter direction to the water in the tubes, toward the front. The hottest water is surrounded by the hottest steam. The hot condensate flows down the curved sides of the Compartment to the condensate line which carries it back to the Auxiliary Heater. Fouling of the compartment with soot while drifting is prevented by the Coffin Air Valve."

Lifting injectors are generally located in front of the cab on the side of the boiler, as on Milwaukee Road 4-6-2 no. 197. This one is a Simplex injector made by Nathan. *Milwaukee Road*

Superheaters

We've talked about making the boiler as efficient as possible by how fuel is used and burned and by raising feedwater temperature. An additional way to increase efficiency is by boosting the temperature of the steam that the boiler produces. Steam produced by the boiler, contained above

The Worthington feedwater heater was an open-type system with multiple components on the locomotive. The heater is atop the smokebox in front of the stack (with piping coming out of it), and the hot-water pump is the boxy structure just above the valve gear (above the second axle of the pilot truck). *Trains magazine collection*

the water in the boiler, is at the boiling temperature (which varies by pressure) and is defined as being saturated—meaning if its temperature is reduced, it will condense back to water.

Superheated steam has been heated above this temperature. When at the same pressure as saturated steam, superheated steam stores greater heat energy in a given volume, which increases the steam's expansive power. This improves efficiency because less steam is required to do the same work within the cylinder. Also, because superheated steam is slower to condense, water from condensation is less likely to form in valve and cylinder chambers.

Superheaters are devices on locomotives that take saturated steam and boost its temperature before routing it to the cylinders. The advent of superheaters brought greatly improved efficiency at relatively low cost and with few negative side effects. A superheated locomotive is more powerful than a comparable engine powered by saturated steam. Notably, superheating didn't add significant size or weight, which allowed railroads to introduce new, more-powerful locomotives without the need to upgrade infrastructure or roundhouse facilities.

The concept of superheating wasn't new, but it wasn't adopted on wide scale in North America until about 1910, when the Schmidt Superheater Company introduced successful equipment. The Schmidt Superheater rapidly became nearly universal and by 1913 most new locomotives were so equipped. This was the most significant locomotive design improvement since Stephenson's *Rocket* because it offered appreciable gains in thermal efficiency without the need for complicated mechanical equipment or an overall increase in locomotive size.

A superheater consists of specially designed tubes that fit into large-diameter boiler flues. Steam from the boiler is routed through the tubes, and the extremely hot gases in the flues (passing from the firebox to the smokebox) raise the steam's temperature by at least 200 degrees (to 600-650 degrees) before it is directed into the cylinders for expansion. This superheated steam has greater expansive power and improves efficiency because less steam is required to do the same work within the cylinder.

Superheating accomplished most of the same goals offered by compounding (more on that in Chaper 7) without the added maintenance. When commercial superheaters became available, railroads pretty much stopped ordering and building compound locomotives (with the exception of a few Mallet articulateds which some lines continued to prefer for heavy, slow-speed work).

Among the complications initially associated with superheating was the need for improved lubricants that could withstand higher temperatures in valve and cylinder friction areas. This initially resulted in some railroads hesitating to adopt superheating, although the problem was soon overcome.

The horizontal cylindrical enclosure identified an Elesco feedwater heater. Size and mounting area varied; this one, on Canadian Pacific 4-6-2 no. 2317, is atop of (and behind the front of) the smokebox. *Brian Solomon*

A common placement for a cylindrical Elesco feedwater heater was on a bracket in front of (and at the top of) the smokebox. This is on New York Central System (Michigan Central) 2-8-2 no. 2019, which is being serviced at the Niles, Mich., roundhouse. *Charles L. Ternes*

Central Vermont 4-6-0 no. 221 features a Coffin feedwater heater mounted over the smokebox ahead of the stack. The semicircular Coffin was easily distinguished from the other commercial varieties of feedwater heaters. *Victor Newton; Robert A. Buck collection*

Boston & Maine ordered 2-8-4 Berkshires from Lima for heavy mainline freight service. These engines employed Coffin feedwater heaters immodestly hung on the front of the locomotive outside the smokebox. *A.S. Arnold*

A related change was the general adoption of piston valves in the place of traditional D-slide valves, as the piston valve proved better suited to superheated steam (more on those in the next chapter).

A typical superheater consists of a header located in the upper portion of the smokebox. This is partitioned with separate passages for incoming saturated steam from the dry pipe and outgoing superheated steam destined for the cylinders. In a Type E superheater, U-shaped tubes are used so the steam makes two passes (forward and back) through each flue; in a Type A, double-U-shaped tubes pass through larger flues, giving steam four passes through each.

These tubes reach to about two feet in front of the back firebox flue sheet. The fronts of the superheater units are shaped to connect to the header. An enclosure built of metal plates protects superheater equipment.

A damper in the smokebox, connected to the steam pipe or steam chest, controls the flow of gases through the large flues that hold the superheater tubes. This damper is closed when the engine is not working steam, and opens when the engine is working.

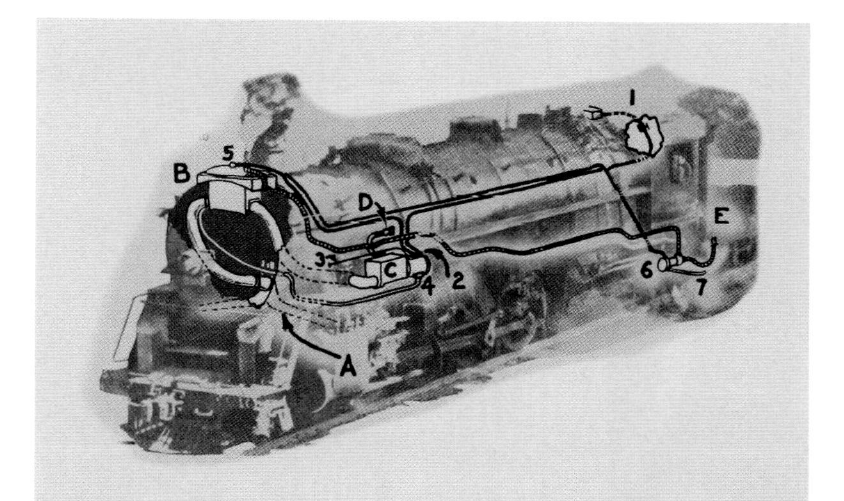

Worthington feedwater heater

The open-system Worthington heater is more complex than closed systems, with components in multiple locations on the locomotive. Here's a basic outline of how it works:

Water from the tender starts at **E**, goes through the cold-water pump (**6**), to the heater (**B**), then through the large pipe to the hot-water pump (**C**)..., and then into the boiler through the check valve (**D**). Exhaust steam goes from the exhaust nozzle **A** to the heater **B**. Live steam runs from a shut-off valve in the cab (**1**) to the hot-water pump (**2**), which is controlled by pilot steam from the engine steam supply so that the pump operates only when the engine is running. Live steam also goes to the water-pump turbine (**6**) by way of the float valve (**5**) which shuts the pump off when water is not needed.

Increasing size and power

All of these technological advancements led to locomotives with increased power. The key that made this worthwhile was the advent of automatic air brakes (see Chapter 5). Prior to air brakes, when brakes were set by brakemen riding atop cars, train size was necessarily small (usually no more than 15-20 cars) and speeds were slow. Automatic air brakes (along with knuckle couplers) allowed longer trains at higher speeds, which quickly pushed an increase in locomotive size starting in the late 1890s.

Through the 1880s, locomotive boilers and fireboxes were small. The firebox was narrow, and had to fit between the driving wheels; typical grate (fire burning surface) area for a 4-4-0 was about 16 to 25 square feet. Boilers were likewise small, with working pressure around 140 to 150 psi. Boilers were small enough to allow windows on the front cab wall above them. Early boilers typically had what is known as a wagon-top shape, with a sharp taper downward in front of the cab and firebox.

By 1900, boilers and fireboxes were growing larger. Boilers were larger in diameter, and were now often straight cylinders ("straight-topped") or gently tapered ("conical"), and their tops approached the level of the cab roof. Working pressure increased to 175 and then 200 psi. Fireboxes likewise increased in size (it takes more heat to boil more water), with typical grate area of 60 to 70 square feet for a 2-6-0 or 4-6-0.

By the 1910s, boilers were as tall as the top of the cab, and working pressure had increased to 225 pounds or more. Fireboxes needed to be larger and wider (grate area of 80-100 square feet), so they either moved atop the drivers—resulting in locomotives with high decks—or were moved behind the drivers, with trailing wheels added to support their weight. This was the start of the modern steam locomotive era.

The Super-Power era

The ultimate culmination in steam locomotive development became known as the Super-Power era, pioneered by William E. Woodward of Lima Locomotive Works in the mid-1920s.

This Illinois Central locomotive has its smokebox door open to reveal the vertical pipe ends of Type A superheater headers extending from the boiler flues. Each superheater element makes two passes inside of the flue that contains it. Below the flues are smaller-diameter tubes. The flues and tubes extend from the firebox through the boiler. The superheater recirculates steam back through the flues to increase its working temperature. *Bruce Meyer*

The builder's plate and superheater plate on Reading & Northern 4-6-2 no. 425 provide clues about the locomotive's history. Number 425 was one of just two 4-6-2s built by Baldwin in January 1928 for Gulf, Mobile & Northern (later part of Gulf, Mobile & Ohio). *Brian Solomon*

Woodward addressed boiler capacity, which had been one of the principal limitations of steam locomotive design. Historically, to compensate for the constraints of boiler capacity, locomotives had been optimized for very specific tasks, typically built for either slow-speed, heavy tonnage trains or hauling comparatively light, fast trains. By designing a larger, more efficient boiler to supply ample quantities of steam at any speed, Woodward aimed to create locomotives that could haul heavier trains at faster sustained speeds.

His designs took advantage of recent efficiency gains made possible by superheaters and feedwater heaters, while introducing significantly larger fireboxes (with grates of 100 square feet and larger) to help support the larger boiler, and also increasing boiler pressure (to 250 and eventually 300 psi) to make more efficient use of steam. To make use of this greater power, Woodward designed large locomotives with greater-diameter driving wheels, while taking advantage of lightweight-alloy steels to reduce the weight of reciprocating parts.

This is a greatly simplified description (entire books have been written about Super-Power development), but it provides an idea of how modern steam locomotives came to be. This evolution also came with a price: boilers had to be stronger; rods, wheels, and other components had to be lighter, stronger, and better balanced; lubricants had to be improved to deal with increased friction and higher temperatures; tenders had to be larger; and many other components had to be refined and upgraded as well.

The result of this development was a series of outstanding locomotives that lived up to the Super-Power name (although other manufacturers didn't use the "Super-Power" term, all began using the fundamental ideas introduced by Lima). Some of the best-known modern locomotives that followed these concepts were Nickel Plate Road's 2-8-4 Berkshires; Chesapeake & Ohio's T-1 2-10-4s; 4-8-4s from New York Central, Union Pacific, and others, and the ultimate in size and power in C&O's Allegheny 2-6-6-6s and UP's 4-8-8-4 Big Boys, both of which were simple articulated locomotives that could move tonnage up heavy grades and at speed.

Now let's move on and look at the valves and cylinders that take the steam and put it into motion.

Chicago, Burlington & Quincy 4-4-0 no. 72 was built at the railroad's Aurora shops in 1878. It has a classic early wagon-top boiler, with firebox located between the drivers. Its firebox grate area was just 16 square feet, with a boiler pressure of 140 psi and 17 x 24-inch cylinders. The small boiler makes the 63" drivers look taller than they are. *Trains magazine collection*

Baldwin built Lehigh & New England 2-8-0 no. 19 in 1905. It has a larger cylindrical boiler; the firebox grate area is 44 square feet with a boiler pressure of 200 psi. It rides on 50" drivers, meaning it's built for power, not speed. *Baldwin*

New York Central Class S-2a 4-8-4 no. 5500 is a thoroughly modern steam locomotive. Built by Alco in 1946, it was the last NYC steam engine produced. It produced 5,000 horsepower, had roller bearings, a grate area of 101 square feet, and boiler pressure of 275 psi. It used Franklin poppet valves instead of conventional piston valves. *Alco*

Chapter 3

Cylinders, valves, and valve gear

Soo Line class H-21 4-6-2 no. 2718 is at Minneapolis on September 14, 1935. Its cylinder cocks are exhausting (note the steam escaping)—an indication that it's just beginning to move forward. It's a classic early 20th century mainline passenger locomotive, well-proportioned with modern features including piston valves and Walschaerts valve gear. *Robert Graham, Brian Solomon collection*

Turning the energy from steam into locomotive motion is the job of the cylinders, pistons, and valves; this machinery is controlled by an intricate system of rods and connectors known as the valve gear. The size and design of these components evolved significantly as builders developed locomotives with more power and increased efficiency.

Most steam locomotives have two cylinders: one on each side of the locomotive, positioned just ahead of the driving wheels. Each cylinder houses a double-acting piston, which as its name implies, provides a power stroke in each direction. Pressurized steam from the boiler is admitted to the cylinder by a valve via back-and-forth motion. This motion is regulated by the valve gear.

Inside the cylinders, energy in the form of pressurized steam is transformed into reciprocating (back-and-forth) motion. The piston transmits the force of expanding steam to a piston rod that extends out of the cylinder. The piston rod is connected via a crosshead to a main rod, which carries that force to the drive wheels, transforming reciprocating action to rotary motion.

Although many of the workings of a steam locomotive are open and visible

Modern steam locomotives had their cylinders cast integral to the locomotive frame. The large bottom opening is the cylinder; the opening directly above it is the valve chamber for the piston valve. The other two openings are for live steam from the boiler and for exhaust steam. The frame is a Southern Pacific 4-8-8-2 under construction. *Baldwin*

Cylinder cross section

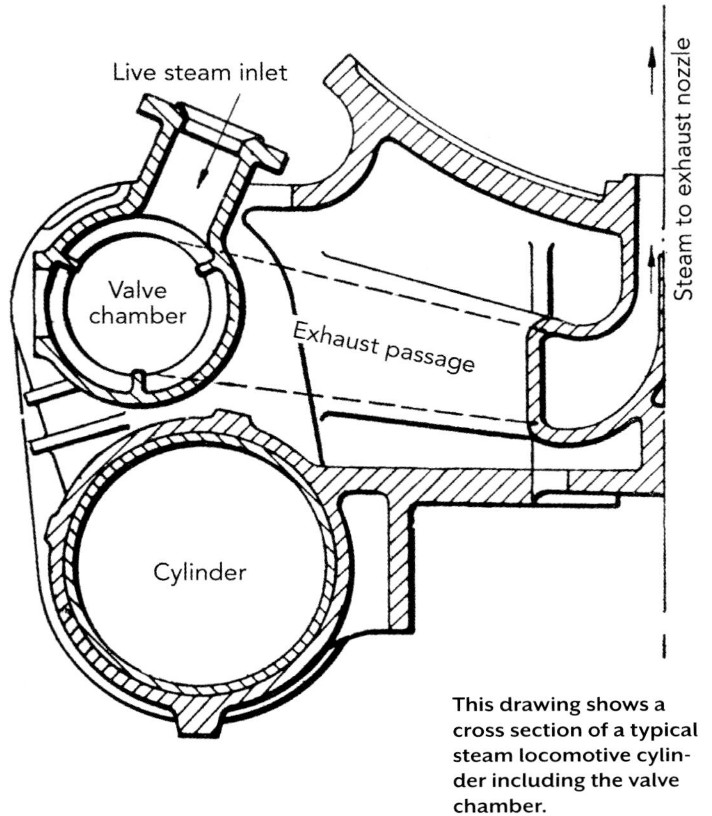

This drawing shows a cross section of a typical steam locomotive cylinder including the valve chamber.
Kalmbach Media

to eye, the workings of the cylinder and valves are necessarily concealed to keep the system "steam-tight." The cylinder and the piston within are fairly simple equipment; visualizing the role they play is fundamental to understanding how a locomotive works. More complicated are the workings of the valves and valve gear, and all of these components are integrally related.

Cylinder arrangement

In steam's formative years a variety of cylinder arrangements were tried in locomotive design. A few very early locomotives employed vertically oriented cylinders, the pistons of which moved rocker arms connected to drive wheels. Other arrangements required geared driving arrangements. However, by far the most successful was the arrangement established by Robert Stephenson's *Rocket*: a pair of cylinders, one on each side of the boiler, directly connected to drive wheels via a main rod.

The *Rocket* featured rear-facing cylinders situated near the firebox end of the boiler, and despite its success, this arrangement was soon reversed, with front-facing cylinders placed near the smokebox at the forward end of the locomotive. Early locomotives tended to use steeply inclined cylinders, partly to keep the cylinders out of the way and above leading wheels. Gradually, cylinders were brought to a level orientation.

An early design practice located cylinders between the locomotive frames and inside the smokebox with connections to drive wheels inside the frame. This once common arrangement was described as "inside-connected with inside cylinders." Among the advantages of this arrangement was energy conservation keeping cylinders

This closeup view (upper left) of recently restored Central of New Jersey 0-6-0 no. 113 shows a cylinder head, which on most locomotives is covered by a cap. Number 113 was built by Alco in 1923 and features 23x26-inch cylinders. The cylinder head is bolted to the end of the cylinder to form a steam-tight space where the piston is acted upon by high-pressure steam.
Brian Solomon

The cylinder's inner details (valve, valve chamber, cylinder, piston, and steam passages) are normally concealed from scrutiny. To give visitors a better understanding of how this machinery works, Steamtown in Scranton, Pa., cut open this casting and painted components to make them more visible. The D-slide valve is the semi-circular component near the top of the casting (below the word "valve")—it is attached to the valve stem (the rod painted white). The piston is the unpainted metal at the far left of the cylinder cutaway. *Brian Solomon*

warm. It involved connecting drive wheels with rods via a cranked axle, which made the inspection and maintenance of cylinders and pistons more difficult. The construction of cranked axles was far more expensive than conventional axles, and the cranked axles were prone to cracking and other structural defects.

As locomotives grew larger and more powerful, the lack of space within the frame limited equipment placement and further complicated maintenance. By the early 1850s, inside-cylinder/inside-connected designs fell out of favor in North America.

Instead, outside-connected locomotives equipped with a pair of forward-facing outside cylinders emerged as the standard arrangement for most North American practice. It would remain so through the end of steam production in the 1950s. There were some notable exceptions, including various types of compound engines, three-cylinder simple engines, and geared locomotive types, each of which will be dealt with in chapters 7 and 8.

Cylinder design and construction

In its established form, the basic locomotive cylinder underwent relatively few changes during the 1800s, but was subject to a variety of improvements in the 1900s that were made possible by improved materials and advanced construction techniques.

In classic locomotive design, cylinders were cast from a hard grade of iron. Castings were relatively complicated as they necessarily included steam admission and exhaust passages. Once cast, cylinders require extensive machining before they are complete. The central portion needs to be bored to form a perfectly cylindrical shape

Cylinders with slide valves can be spotted by the box-like enclosure for the valve atop the cylinder. This is on Northern Pacific 4-6-0 no. 328, built by Alco in 1907. *Trains magazine collection*

Steam (Cylinder) Admission Valves

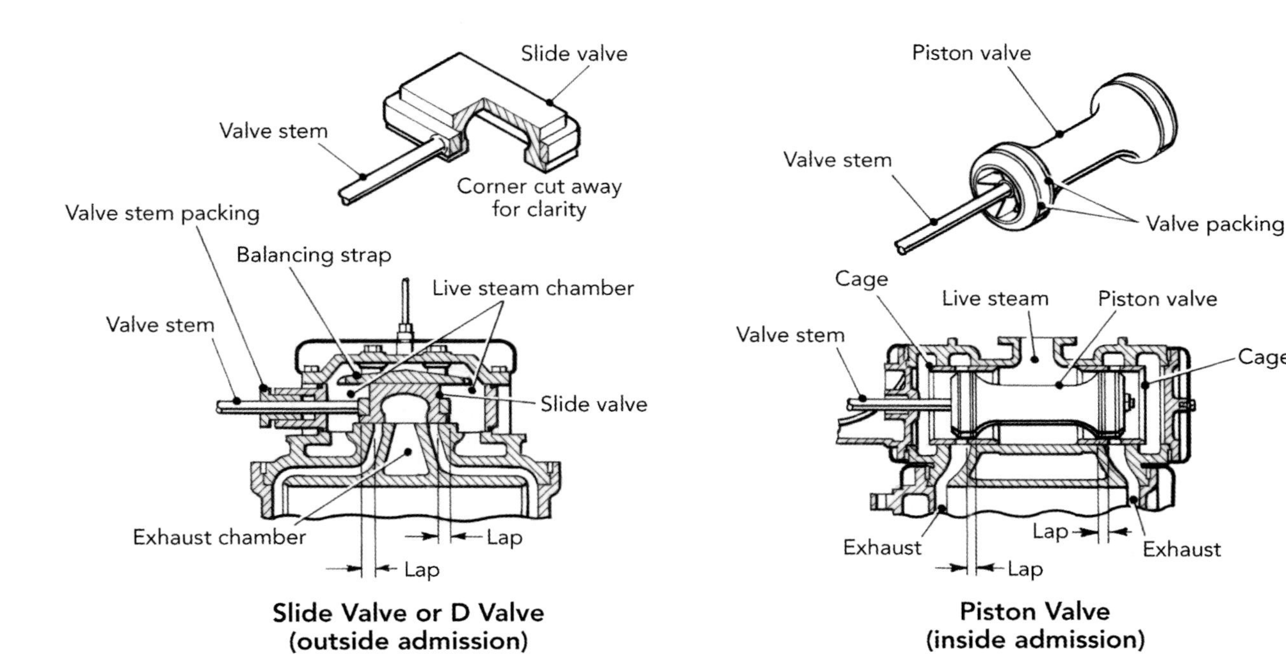

The most common locomotive valves were the slide (D valve) and the spool-shaped, cylindrical piston valve. *Kalmbach Media*

to match the piston and insure a tight fit. Cylinder ends require turning, ports and passages need to be finished, and valve seats were planed smooth with a surface matching valve faces. Cylinder heads were fitted at each end and bolted tightly into place to ensure a steam-tight fit.

Typically, cylinders were secured to the locomotive through frame-mounted supports called cylinder saddles. A common variation to this design involved a half-saddle arrangement, where one cylinder was cast together with half the saddle, and the two cylinder-saddle castings were fabricated together during construction. After the introduction of affordable mass-produced steel making, cast steel was commonly substituted for cast iron in cylinder construction, yet cast-iron liners were still necessary.

In the 1920s, advances in casting permitted cylinders to be cast integrally with locomotive frames. This became a standard feature of many late-era locomotives, and was often noted for locomotives exhibiting exceptional performance.

To conserve energy and minimize the risk of burning anyone bumping the cylinder, cylinders were often covered in cylinder lagging (insulation) and encased in a metal cylinder casing. Early cylinder casing was often fabricated from polished Russia iron; in the wood burning-era, when locomotives enjoyed elaborate decoration, it wasn't unusual for cylinder casing to be made from brass with highly polished caps over the cylinder heads. Although attractive, these embellishments disguised the working cylinder. By the late 1800s, ornamentation had largely disappeared, and the cylinder casing took on a more utilitarian form.

Cylinder size

Cylinder dimensions are among the most commonly quoted locomotive specifications and are a key determining indicator of its power potential. Steam cylinder size is typically listed in inches by bore diameter

On May 4, 1957, one of Pennsylvania's late class I1s 2-10-0s leads a northward train out of Max siding on the Elmira Branch near Trout Run, Pa. These locomotives had small drivers and limited maximum cut-off, and were extremely powerful.
Jim Shaughnessy, collection of the Center for Railroad Photography & Art

Northern Pacific 4-6-2 no. 2108, built by Schenectady in 1904, is an example of a locomotive built during the transitional developmental phase in the early 20th century when piston valves were coming into favor, but before the adoption of outside valve gear. This locomotive uses an angled valve arrangement so that the valve stems can reach connections to Stephenson gear located inside the engine frame.
Brian Solomon collection

and length of piston stroke. For example, a 25 x 28 cylinder has a 25"-diameter cylinder with a 28"-long stroke.

As with internal-combustion engines, piston and cylinder size is directly related to power: more-powerful locomotives have larger cylinders. Light locomotives assigned to switching services had the smallest cylinders, while heavy freight locomotives designed for moving tonnage on steep grades had the largest cylinders. Locomotive cylinder sizes in general grew significantly from the late 1800s through the end of the steam era.

Cylinder dimensions were tailored to individual locomotive classes according to common formulas. Heavy freight engines were characterized by large-diameter cylinders with long strokes; in the 1900s these ranged from 28" to 32" in diameter with a 30" to 34" stroke. Traditionally, engines designed for fast service, especially passenger locomotives, benefited from a shorter piston stroke, rarely more than 24" in the 19th century. Late-era passenger locomotives benefited from longer strokes, such as the Norfolk & Western J Class 4-8-4s, which featured 27 x 32 cylinders.

The largest cylinders were used by compound locomotives for their low-pressure engines, where the power output of low-pressure cylinders was roughly matched to corresponding high-pressure cylinders. The most extreme example was on massive 2-10-10-2 Mallet compounds built for Virginian that featured 48"-diameter low-pressure cylinders on the forward engine (see Chapter 7 for detailed information on compounds).

Valves

The key to control and operation of the cylinders are the valves that regulate the admission of steam and rid the cylinder of exhaust in a controlled sequence; the actual sequencing of the valves is performed by valve gear. The valve is typically housed in either a chamber or bore directly atop the cylinder.

In the 19th century the most common type of valve was the D-style slide valve, so-called because the shape of the valve's longitudinal profile resembled a capital letter D face down against the valve-seat atop the cylinder (see the drawing atop page 75). The valve was housed in a steam chest and

Valve and cylinder operation

This series of drawings shows how link motion and valve movement regulates steam admission to the piston. Red is incoming steam from the dry pipe; gray is spent steam to be exhausted. (The drawings show Walschaerts valve gear; others provide similar valve/piston motion.)

View A shows valve gear with the radius rod lifted for reverse motion. In B and C, the radius rod is fully down for maximum power at full cutoff. Views D to H show a complete motion cycle for forward movement (at about 50 percent cutoff).

typically consisted of two castings: a squared iron box machined with steam-tight surface to match the valve seat and a cast-iron cover bolted in place over it. The valve is attached to a valve stem actuated by the valve gear. As the valve slides back and forth, it opens and closes ports to the cylinder. In its common applications, the D-slide valve is an example of an outside-admission valve.

The D-slide valve was prized for its simplicity, low initial cost, and ease of operation, but it suffered from high wear between the valve and valve seat, and it proved difficult to lubricate. Wear resulted from high friction caused by steam pressure on the top of the valve. On early locomotives, lubrication for slide valves was provided by an ordinary oil cup that rode on top of the valve. Later, more involved systems of hydrostatic lubrication resulted in longer valve life.

Various design improvements aimed to produce what was known as a "balanced slide valve," which attempted to obviate difficulties associated with valve friction and related high wear problems that limited valve life and lowered engine efficiency. However, the significantly higher cost of balanced slide valves and their greater complexity precluded widespread adoption.

The solution proved to be the spool-shaped piston valve. It had been developed in the mid-19th century and was initially applied to limited degree on specialized locomotive types, notably Baldwin's Vauclain compound. The piston valve employed a symmetrically shaped valve with pistons positioned opposite one another on a common spindle. In later years this typically used a hollow arrangement with

This late-era Boston & Maine P4a 4-6-2 shows off its Walschaerts valve gear, 23x28-inch cylinders, and 80" drivers. It was built by Lima in 1934. It's shown in service at Rigby Yard in South Portland, Maine; it now resides at Steamtown in Scranton, Pa. *George C. Corey*

933

Boston & Maine no. 933 is an example of a mid-1890s 4-4-0 that was upgraded to more-modern standards. It was built by Manchester Locomotive Works and later rebuilt with piston valves and a superheater. It retained its inside Stephenson valve gear. It's in Boston in April 1939. *Robert A. Buck collection*

Stephenson valve gear

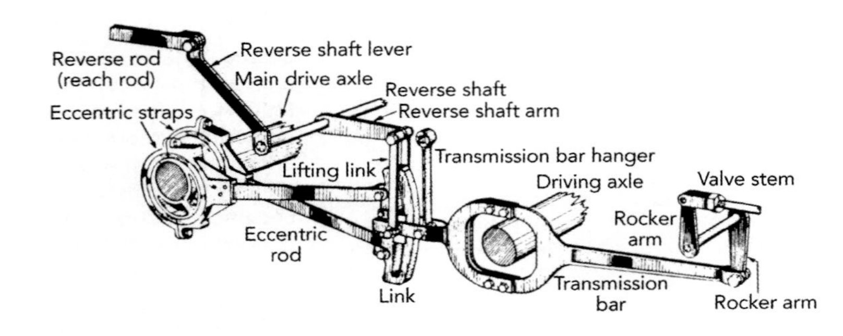

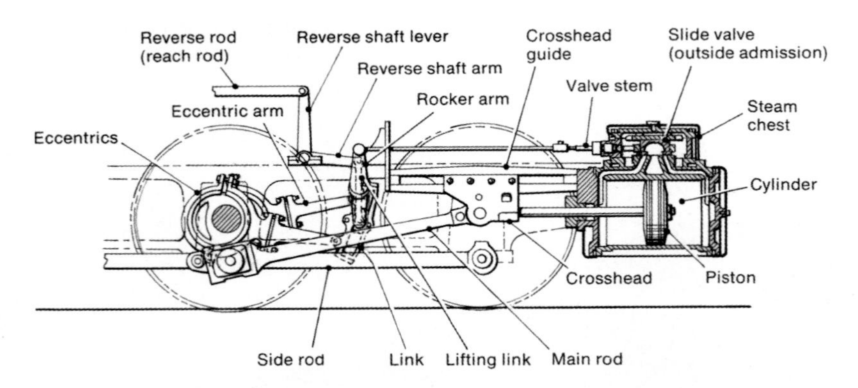

inside admission, whereby live steam acted upon the inside piston faces.

Piston valves became standard equipment in the early 20th century, especially when railroads embraced superheated steam. The problem of effectively lubricating D-slide valves was made worse when exposed to the hotter superheated steam. As a result the traditional slide valve rapidly fell out of favor. By World War I, piston valves had supplanted the older valve type on most new road locomotives.

Valves at work

In a typical locomotive, steam enters a cylinder through a pair of inlet ports with exhaust being released via a single exhaust port. The piston within the cylinder is double acting; so as steam is admitted to one half of the cylinder, the other half is simultaneously exhausting condensing gases.

Additional ports, known as cylinder cocks, are controlled manually from the locomotive cab and used when starting the locomotive to evacuate any condensed water that may have accumulated in the cylinder. Water cannot be compressed and thus must be expelled from the cylinder to mitigate the risk of damage to the cylinder, the cylinder heads, and the piston. In extreme situations, water accumulating in the cylinder can result in the cylinder head blowing out or the cylinder casting cracking.

Cylinder valve events must be carefully sequenced and timed in the correct order for the locomotive to work efficiently. This includes the timing of steam admission to the cylinder, the steam admission cutoff (the point when steam stops entering the cylinder), the timing of exhaust, and the moment of compression.

Since the valve passages and cylinder ports are fixed in place, the timing and control of valve motion as regulated by the valve gear is adjusted to control the power and speed of the engine. The specific workings of various types of valve gear are detailed later in this chapter.

Valves are set to begin steam admission just before the start of the piston stroke. This timing is necessary both to provide desired expansive force during the early part of the stroke and also to provide a degree of compressive resistance at the end of the of the stroke to prevent unnecessary wear or damage between the piston and cylinder head. As steam ports are opened on the admission end of the cylinder, exhaust ports are opened on the exhaust end to evacuate steam from that end of the piston. As the piston is forced away from one end of the cylinder to the other, steam continues to be admitted into the cylinder behind it, but at some point admission ports are closed to cut off the flow of steam. However, the steam continues to expand within the cylinder until the cycle reverses at the end of the stroke, and the whole process repeats, but in the opposite direction.

The length of steam admission during stroke is described as the "cutoff," a term derived from the action of ending or "cutting off" the steam jet. The ability to vary the cutoff—in other words, controlling the length of steam admission—is accomplished by closing the admission port, and this is a principle means of controlling the power and speed of a steam engine, and it is regulated by manipulation of valve gear.

A locomotive's pistons, cylinders, connecting rods, and driving wheels are connected to one another in a fixed relationship, so the length of the cutoff is one of the only variable controls available during operation. The other control is the throttle, which is used to regulate the volume of steam entering the cylinders.

To operate the engine at maximum power, the valves are set for their longest travel, which means they are adjusted to expose the cylinder admission ports for the greatest portion of the stroke and thus allow more steam to enter the cylinder. This position is called "maximum cutoff" or "full stroke" (and has been described as working the engine in "full gear"). On traditional engines, the maximum cutoff may be up to 85-90 percent of the length of the stroke. (Because steam needs to expand to do its work, there is no benefit in applying steam for 100 percent of the stroke—doing so would have negative effects because the inability for expanding steam to exit the cylinder quickly at the end of the stroke would impede the piston thrust and reduce the power of the engine.)

Working the locomotive at maximum cutoff will produce the maximum tractive effort possible—similar to a heavy truck in low gear. Although this is often necessary to get a train started, once the locomotive begins to gain speed, the engineer must shorten the cutoff (reduce steam admission to a shorter part of the stroke) to continue to get the best performance from the locomotive.

When the valves are set at maximum cutoff, the engine exhausts a large volume of steam into the atmosphere before it expands, and when steam under high pressure escapes through the stack it results in a distinct barking sound. Unnecessarily working an

Its cylinder cocks open, Valley Railroad no. 40 has just begun to move, offering a good view of its Walschaerts valve gear. This gear employed a radial slotted rocking link mounted on a fixed central fulcrum (above the second driver). Primary motion is via the link connected to a main driver crank arm (out of sight to the right) that is set 90 degrees off axis from the cylinder. Secondary motion regulating valve lap and lead is derived from the crosshead connection (clearly shown in this image as the rod network connected to the crosshead outside the crosshead guides) that joins the primary motion link above the end of the valve stem. To adjust valve travel and set the direction of the engine, the engineer uses the reverser to raise or lower the stationary link block (at the top of the rocking link) from the center position. Here the stationary link is raised. *Brian Solomon*

Walschaerts valve gear

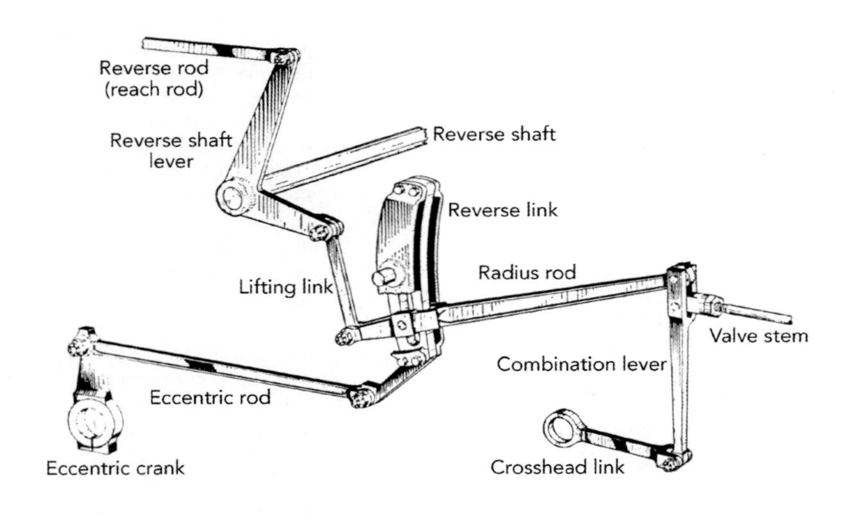

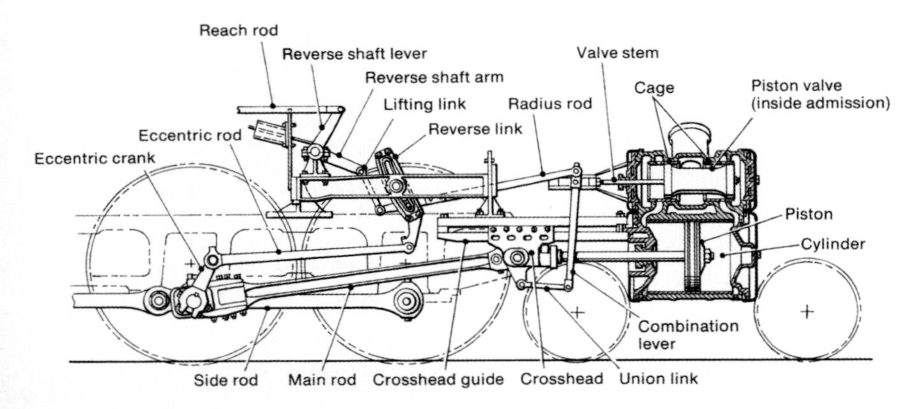

engine at maximum cutoff is inefficient and wastes fuel and water. It also produces back pressure on the piston during the return stroke as a result of expanding steam that cannot be evacuated quickly enough through exhaust ports, limiting the ability of the engine to accelerate.

By shortening the cutoff, the engineer limits the quantity of steam entering the cylinder. This gives it greater room to expand and allows it to exhaust at a lower pressure. The ability to shorten the cutoff depends on the design of the engine and the nature of its intended service. On traditionally designed engines, cutoff may be shortened to 20-25 percent of the stroke. On modern fast passenger locomotives, the engineer could shorten the cutoff to just a small fraction of the piston stroke, with some advanced valve designs allowing just a 5 percent cutoff at top speeds.

Designers took great pains in calculating optimal timing for valve events when developing locomotives. Steam admission and cutoff points were carefully planned. Period trade literature explored at length discussions of steam admission diagrams that aimed to optimize cylinder proportions, the size and placement of cylinder ports, and the length and rate of valve travel. Successfully optimizing valve events played an important role in tailoring a locomotive to its maximum speed and power output and most-efficient fuel consumption.

To improve efficiency, some later-era steam locomotives were designed with a limited maximum cutoff of just 50-60 percent, which required auxiliary starting ports to allow full cutoff for situations where the engine was near center and unable to get started. A classic example of a locomotive designed with a limited maximum cutoff was Pennsylvania Railroad's class I1s 2-10-0. These big-boilered, superheated freight haulers featured relatively small drivers and were nicknamed "Hippos" because of their appearance. As built, the I1s weighed 386,100 pounds and featured 50 percent maximum cutoff; tractive effort was listed at 90,000 pounds. According to *Pennsy Power* by Al Staufer, when PRR tested I1s no. 790 at the Altoona test plant it demonstrated extraordinary power and relative efficiency: when working at full throttle at 7 mph, it delivered 41 percent more horsepower than the railroad's class L1s 2-8-2, while consuming 12 percent less steam.

Valve gear

Angus Sinclair wrote in his early 20th century history of the locomotive, *The Development of the Locomotive Engine*, "[w]e do not know of any subject that excites so much interest among the rank and file of railroad mechanical men as valve motions." Yet, in the study of locomotive working, operation of the valve gear typically eludes most modern observers.

It is indeed a complex subject. You don't need to understand the exact workings of valve gear at the level of a mechanical engineer, and if some of the descriptions are difficult to grasp, that's OK. At its simplest, you just need to understand two basic things. First, the reverse lever isn't simply a forward/neutral/reverse control like gears on an automobile or truck. The reverse lever is a full quadrant, adjustable from full forward through neutral and full reverse. Second, when the engineer moves the reverse lever forward and backward, it moves a system of rods and levers that regulate valve travel, which does two things: tells the locomotive to go forward or in reverse, and sets the amount of cutoff as described earlier.

By regulating the passage of steam to and from the cylinders, the engineer controls the locomotive's speed, power, and ultimately the efficiency of its operation. The term "gear" describes the assembled machinery used to transmit motion and change the rate of motion in regard to sequencing valves that admit and exhaust steam from the cylinders. Typically it consists of rods, links, and eccentrics that derive motion from the locomotive running gear.

In 19th century design, most locomotives used inside valve gear, so called because it was located inside the locomotive frame and between the drive wheels of the locomotive. In its most common form, inside gear takes its motion from cam-actuated eccentrics riding on the main driving axle. Although many master mechanics of the period prided themselves in valve gear design and many different types of valve gear were applied, the most common type of inside valve gear was the Stephenson link (page 82).

Yet, when valve gear is hidden between the drivers it is difficult for observers to appreciate the details of how it works when the engine is in motion.

By contrast, outside valve gear, positioned outside the locomotive frames and beyond the driving wheels, is easily observed. Several common types were employed that take motion from crankpin-mounted eccentrics and/or crosshead connections. Outside valve gear became standard by the early 1900s as locomotives grew larger and had less room between drivers for the cams, eccentrics, and other components. Inside gear was also more difficult to maintain. In general the trend

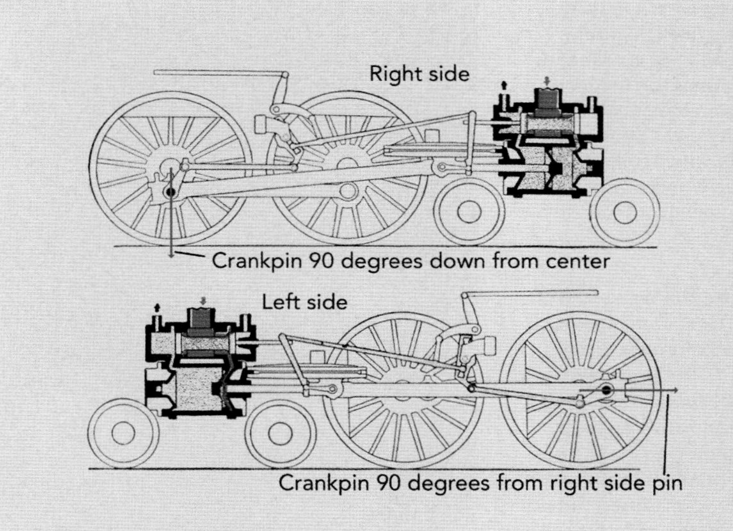

Driver quartering

A challenge in designing and operating a steam locomotive is that when the locomotive begins moving and the main rod acts on the crankpin of the driver, it can't move the locomotive if the pin is "dead centered"—when the crankpin is farthest away or closest to the piston (as on the bottom illustration). To offset this, the crankpins on opposite sides of a locomotive are rotated 90 degrees from each other (called "quartering"). This way, the main rod on both sides can't be dead centered at the same time.

In the top illustration, on the right-hand side of the locomotive, the main crankpin is at a 90 degree angle from horizontal compared to the wheel center. On the left-hand side, the main crank is horizontal with the wheel center, meaning it is rotated 90 degrees from the crank on the right side.

to adopt outside gear coincided with the adoption of larger, more-powerful engine designs.

Walschaerts was the first common design of outside valve gear, and became the most widely used. Other outside valve gear developed to improve efficiency included the Baker, Southern, and Young designs. Of these, the Baker and Southern were similar to Walschaerts and Stephenson because they derived valve motion from an eccentric crank located on the end of the crankpin of the main driver; the Young was unusual in that it derived valve motion

New York Central 4-8-2 Mohawk no. 3100, built by Lima during World War II, exhibits a late-era arrangement featuring piston valves, multiple-bearing crosshead, Worthington feedwater heater, Baker valve gear, lightweight alloy steel rods, and Scullin Disc drive wheels. *Trains magazine collection*

Here's the Walschaerts valve gear arrangement on a Baltimore & Ohio 4-6-2. The union link (the lower link parallel with piston rod) transmits lead motion via the perpendicular combination lever (positioned outside the piston rod and crosshead) to a junction with the radius rod and valve stem. *James P. Gallagher*

entirely from crosshead connections.

The series of illustrations on page 78 shows how steam travels and how valves work as the locomotive wheels turn. The example uses Walschaerts gear, but the basic principles apply regardless of valve gear type.

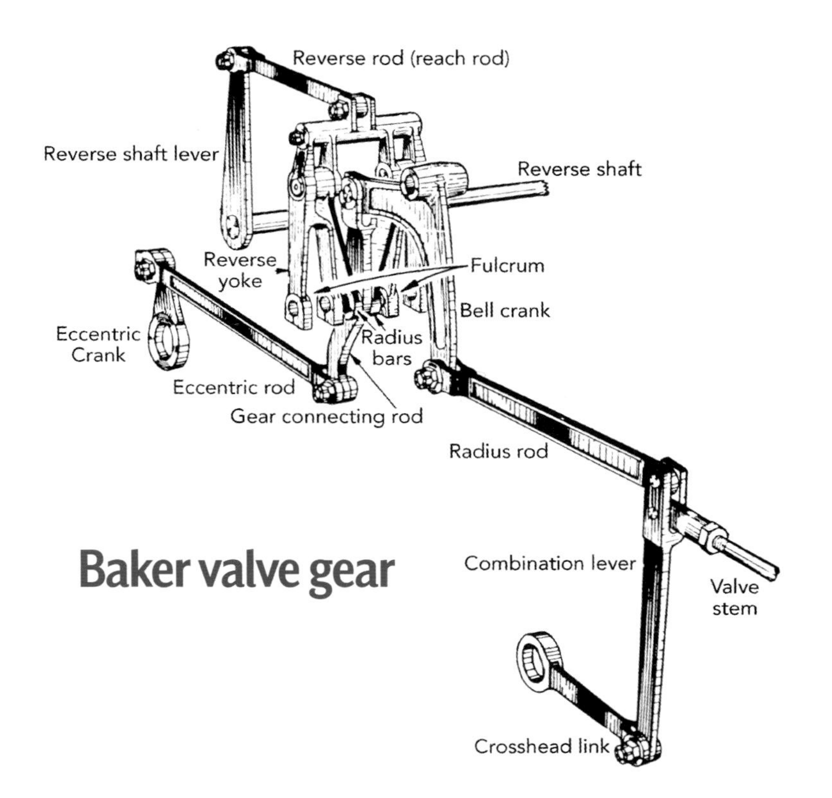

Baker valve gear

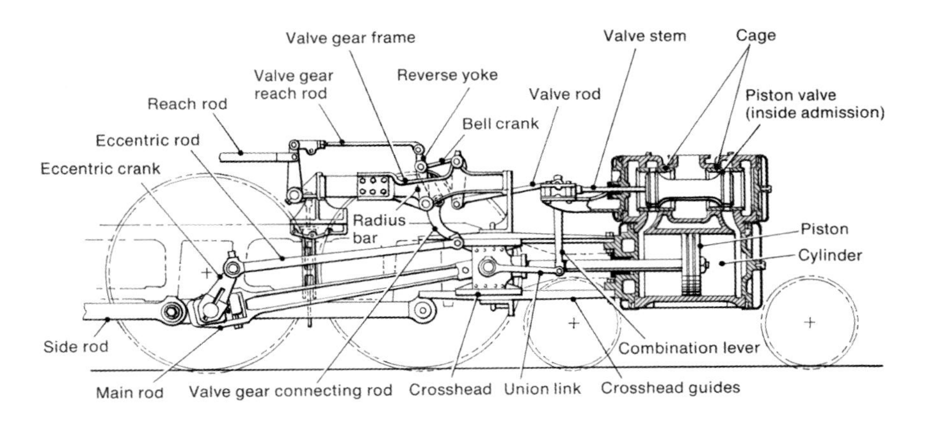

Stephenson link

As noted, Stephenson valve gear is an inside type, located inside the frame. The Stephenson gear features a pair of eccentrics for each cylinder. These are attached via cams to the main driving axle and connect to eccentric rods. One eccentric/eccentric-rod combination is for forward motion, the other for reverse. The rods connect to a link that is used to engage or disengage them one at a time to a rocker. The link is the adjustable component controlled by the engineer using the reverser to alter the motion of the valve gear to adjust valve travel. Control is by raising or lowering the link to engage and adjust the amount of travel of either the forward or reverse eccentric rods. The link connects via an arrangement of rods and a rocker to the valve stem and thus moves the slide valve back and forth. Relative adjustments to the link can be used to shorten or lengthen valve travel as a means to control the amount of steam entering the cylinder during the length of the stroke.

If the engineer puts the reverser to "full forward" (maximum cutoff), the forward eccentric rod is engaged and the link is moved to its most extreme position relative to the forward rod. This sets the valves to admit steam throughout the greatest possible length of the piston stroke. As the engineer moves the reverser back toward the center position, the link shortens the cutoff, admitting steam for only a corresponding portion of the stroke, reducing the amount of steam entering the cylinder. At center, the engine is in the neutral position, and neither eccentric rod is engaged so no steam is admitted to the cylinders.

The Stephenson design was widely used until the turn of the 20th century, and although it worked well, maintenance and access issues led it to fall out of favor as locomotives became more powerful. There was no practical way to apply the Stephenson design as an outside gear, so builders turned to other types. Few locomotives were built with Stephenson gear after 1910.

Chessie System
2101

Former Reading T-1 no. 2101 works as the Chessie Steam Special at the horseshoe curve in Mance, Pa., on ascent of the Baltimore & Ohio grade to Sand Patch. The engineer has no. 2101 in full forward gear—the valves are set to allow maximum steam admission into the cylinders—as evident by the Baker Valve gear reverse arm lowered to its most extreme position (at top left of the first drive wheel). This is needed on the steep grade, made worse by the light rain making the rails slippery. *George W. Kowanski*

Strasburg Railroad 4-8-0 no. 475 is equipped with Baker valve gear. Baker is similar to Walschaerts; however, to adjust valve travel, Baker uses a large double-bell crank-rocker in place of the Walshaerts connection. The reverser adjusts the crank rocker up or down to adjust valve travel. The crank rocker is visible at center to the right and above the main-rod connection on the crosshead. *Pat Yough*

Southern Railway 2-8-0 no. 630 features the relatively rare Southern valve gear. It is similar to Walchaerts but without clumsy crosshead connections; instead, it derives motion from a driver-driven return crank. It regulates valve motion via a bell-crank connection to the valve stem. The type is readily identifiable by the pair of vertical rods at the center of the mechanism that connect the horizontally oriented eccentric rod to the guide block (to the left of the crosshead). *Pat Yough*

Walschaerts valve gear

Walschaerts valve gear was invented by Egide Walschaerts, a Belgian, in 1844. The first U.S. use was on Mason Bogie locomotives in the 1870s. It gained large popularity just after 1900, eventually becoming the most-common outside valve gear used in the U.S. (see page 84).

One set of Walschaerts (outside) gear is located on each side of the locomotive to regulate the valves on that side. Primary motion, used for controlling the steam port opening, is from a main driver crank arm and eccentric that is set 90 degrees off axis from the main rod linkage (the main rod transmits the piston thrust via the crosshead to the main driver). A rod reaching from the crank arm connects to the radial slotted rocking link that is mounted on a fixed central fulcrum, on which a stationary link block may be raised or lowered by the engineer using the reverser—this operates a lifting arm and lifting link.

A connection called the radius rod transmits primary motion from the stationary link to the valve stem via a linkage to the connecting rod called the combination lever (used to link with secondary motion described below) that joins via a valve spindle crosshead. The gear's secondary motion, used to regulate valve lap and lead, is derived from a crosshead connection through a rod network outside the crosshead guides. This secondary linkage joins the primary motion via the combination lever that connects with the radius rod above the end of the valve spindle connection.

To adjust valve travel and set the direction of the engine, the engineer uses the reverser to move the network of connections that raises or lowers the lifting arm and lifting link, which changes the relative

Southern valve gear

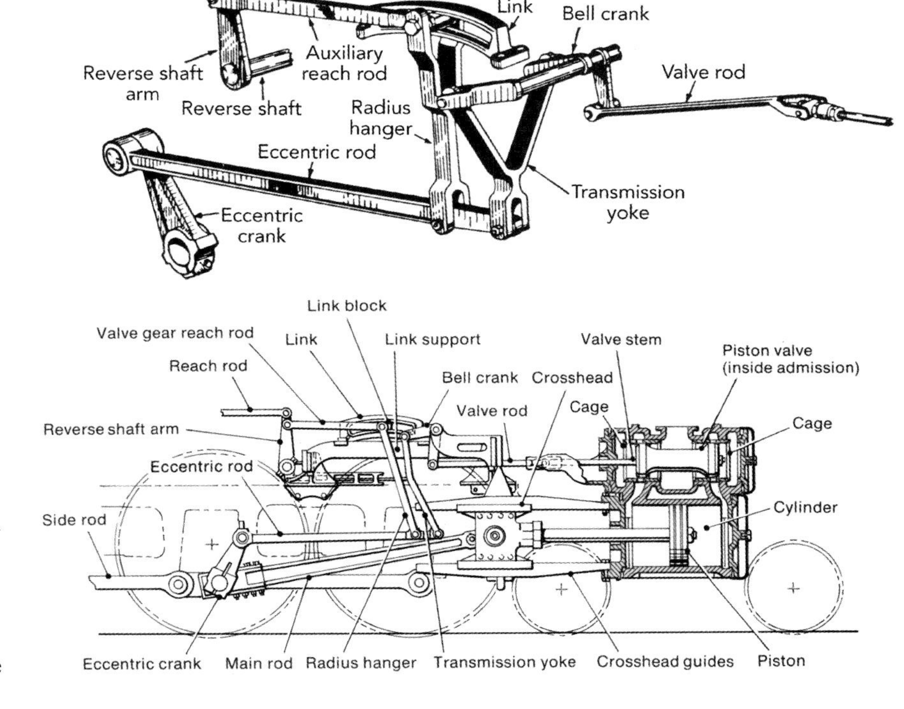

Union Pacific 2-10-2 no. 5519 is equipped with distinctive Young valve gear. Note the twin reach rods and the lack of an eccentric rod and crank. The locomotive was built by Baldwin in 1924; it's shown here in 1940.
G. Best

Gresley conjugated valve gear

Large three-cylinder locomotives faced special challenges regarding design and location of valve gear. In the 1920s, Alco promoted its powerful three-cylinder locomotives as a means of more efficiently moving heavy trains. These locomotives used an adaptation of the Gresley conjugated valve gear developed in England by London & North Eastern Railway's Nigel Gresley (later knighted, becoming Sir Nigel Gresley) initially for application on fast 4-6-2 Pacifics.

Gresley's gear was designed to control valve sequencing on a middle cylinder of a simple three-cylinder locomotive. The middle cylinder powered a crank axle and required unusually tight space constraints. The arrangement of outside cylinders followed well-established practice with main drive rods connecting the crosshead with crankpins on a second driving axle using typical Walschaerts valve gear.

Ordinarily, valves are situated directly above the cylinder they regulate. However, in order to keep the central cylinder valve on a level plane with the valves of the outside cylinders, Gresley oriented the central valve adjacent to the cylinder rather than above it. Since the space between the drive wheels precluded use of conventional Walschaerts gear for the central cylinder, Gresley designed a style of conjugated gear that derives its motion by combining the events of the two outside Walschaerts gears.

This is a distinctly different sort of

Union Pacific's 4-12-2s, built by Alco, were the largest class of three-cylinder locomotives built in the U.S. They featured a high-capacity boiler that supplied two outside cylinders (connected to the second driving axle in the conventional) and a middle cylinder with inside rod via an inside crank to the second axle. Gresley conjugated valve gear was used to govern steam admission to the middle cylinder. The gear and middle cylinder of no. 9051 can be seen just below the smokebox. *George C. Corey*

The front frame casting for the UP 4-12-2 includes the two outside cylinders along with the opening (middle) for the front (third) cylinder.

A cranked axle was used for the front cylinder to turn the lead pair of drivers.

valve gear. Unlike conventional radial valve gears (which derive motion from eccentrics connected to driving wheels/axles) it instead consists of a network of levers situated at the front of the engine ahead of the cylinders that are moved by valve spindle extensions from valves above outside cylinders. A key to the operation of the Gresley gear is a large, laterally oriented two-to-one lever (the ratio of the lengths from the levers' pivoting fulcrum), which connects at the long end to a valve spindle extension, with the short end connected to the fulcrum point of a short equal lever (a lever with equal lengths from its pivot point). At one end the equal lever connects with the valve spindle on the opposite outside cylinder, while the other end connects to central valve-spindle. The resulting back-and-forth motion of the equal lever is what controls the steam admission to the central valve. While this may sound somewhat complicated, the Gresley conjugated valve gear is remarkably simple in operation.

Alco applied this to a range of its three-cylinder locomotives, most notably the massive 4-12-2s built for Union Pacific between 1926 and 1930. Although the Gresley conjugated gear had its difficulties, UP's locomotives worked in their as-built condition for three decades, demonstrating the durability of this gear when properly maintained.

Few three-cylinder locomotives were built; the emergence of Super-Power principles to locomotive design resulted in very powerful two-cylinder conventional locomotives without the need for additional mechanical components of a third cylinder.

Young valve gear

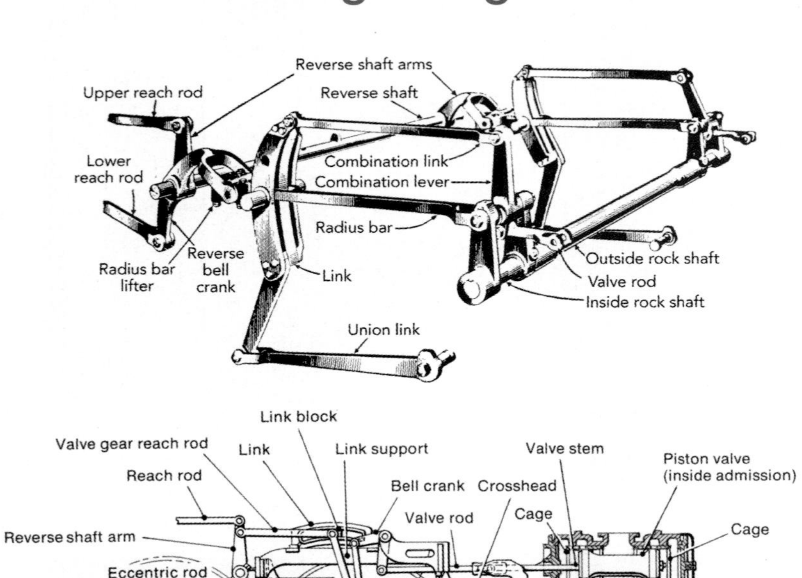

position of the stationary link block. As with the Stephenson link, the center position is neutral. Raising the rocking link will set the engine in motion in one direction, lowering below center will reverse it.

Baker valve gear

The Baker design (page 87) is a Walschaerts variation invented by A.D. Baker in 1903 and introduced to North American practice in 1908. It was widely produced by the Pilliod Company of New York. Baker uses a similar motion to Walschaerts, except that it employs a distinctive bell-shaped rocker crank to adjust valve travel. This obviated the need for the link and block. To move the engine forward, the engineer moves the reverser forward to lower the reverse arm and lower the bell crank. To move the engine backward, the reverser is pulled back, which raises the bell crank.

The engineer of Rock Island 2-8-2 no. 2684 has opened the cylinder cocks and cracked the throttle, and water vapor blasts from its cylinders as the massive machine begins to move away from the turntable. Purging this moisture is vital to avoid damaging the piston and cylinder. *Robert A. Witbeck, collection of the Center for Railroad Photography & Art*

On early locomotives, the reverse lever directly controlled the linkage. As locomotives became bigger, power reverse mechanisms—using steam or air—were implemented to make it physically easier to move the lever. This is a power reverse on Milwaukee Road 4-6-4 no. 6414 in 1931. *Milwaukee Road*

Another advantage, touted in Pilliod's ads, was that the use of this gear doesn't depend upon the size or type of locomotive or the location of the valve gear on the locomotive. Alfred Bruce in *The Steam Locomotive in America* wrote that the advantage of Baker gear was that "all wearing surfaces are made up of pins and bushings, and standardization and replacement of worn parts are achieved in a very simple and inexpensive manner—by means of new pins and bushings." Although Baker valve gear enjoyed many late-era applications (it was found on more than 14,000 locomotives by 1938), it was never as common as Walschaerts.

Southern and Young valve gears

Southern valve gear was not common, but was the third-most-used modern valve gear behind Walschaerts and Baker. It was patented by William Sherman Brown in 1912. Brown was a Southern Railway engineer, hence the name. It was most common on that railroad's locomotives, but used by others as well. It was similar to Baker gear, but took all its motion from the eccentric crank, eliminating the connection to the crosshead. The radius hanger on the Southern gear performed the same function as the reverse yoke of Baker.

Young valve gear, patented by Otis W. Young, was comparatively rare, and first appeared in 1915. It eliminated the eccentric crank and rod, instead using the motion from one side of the locomotive to drive the valves on the other (made possible because drivers on opposite sides are "quartered," or positioned 90 degrees in relation to the other side—see page 85). The most notable appearances of Young gear were on Union Pacific 2-10-2s and 4-8-2s as built (the 4-8-2s were later rebuilt with Walschaerts gear).

The next chapter will look at rods, crossheads, and wheels, and we'll see how the engine's motion is applied to wheels to make the locomotive move.

Chapter 4

Crossheads, rods, and wheels

Powerful late-era locomotives, such as this Northern Pacific 4-8-4, benefited from lightweight steel-alloy drive rods, main rods, and valve gear components to reduce unbalanced reciprocating weight.
Trains magazine collection

The last few chapters explained how the power of steam is harnessed and turned into reciprocating motion by pistons inside the cylinders. Now we'll look at the components that turn this back-and-forth movement into rotary action of the wheels, putting the locomotive in motion.

Opposite top: Mid- to late-1800s 4-4-0 designs favored the four-bar crosshead, such as locomotive no. 17 *York*, a replica locomotive built in 2013 representing Rogers Locomotive and Machine Works Civil War-era construction. The four-bar arrangement provided clearance for the rear wheels of the leading truck. *Oren B. Helbok*

Several components are involved. The piston rod, which extends from the piston out of the cylinder, is connected to the crosshead, making it slide horizontally back and forth on a hanger. The crosshead provides a pivoting connection to the main rod, which in turn is connected to the main driving wheel at the crank pin, turning it. Motion is transferred from the main driving wheel to the other drivers via one or more side rods. These are the basics; as with other steam operations, putting this sequence of movement into practice is a bit more complex. Here's how they work.

Crosshead

The crosshead is a crucial component in transmitting motion and power from the pistons to the drivers, providing the necessary linkage and pivot point between the piston rod and the main rod. The crosshead itself is a cast-iron block that slides back and forth on crosshead guides. It serves to keep angled torque away from the piston rod, keeping it and the piston firmly in their desired alignment inside the cylinder while providing the important pivot point for the main rod, which is constantly changing its angle as result of the rotation of the drive wheel when the locomotive is in motion. The main rod is attached to the crosshead via a wrist pin.

The crosshead and crosshead guides rely on perfectly matched and finely machined surfaces between them to keep wear to an absolute minimum. The guides are firmly

The crosshead (the heavy casting at left) rides back and forth on the crosshead guides (the horizontal arms at top and bottom. It serves as the connection between the main rod (at far left) and the piston rod (horizontal rod at middle), which extends out from the piston inside the cylinder (at far right). The locomotive is Rio Grande 2-8-0 class C-19 no. 346, built by Baldwin in July 1881. *Brian Solomon*

attached to the locomotive frame using a guide yoke.

In *Catechism of the Locomotive,* Matthias M. Forney wrote, "The guides are set with great care, so as to be exactly parallel with the axis or center line of the cylinder, so that the crosshead will slide in exactly the same path that the piston-rod will if it moves in a straight line. If the piston rod and the [main rod] are attached to the crosshead, all the strain produced by the obliquity of the [main rod] will be borne by the guides, thus relieving the piston-rod, and making certain it will move in a straight line."

The basic principle of the crosshead guide changed very little over the evolution of the steam locomotive, but over the years various patterns and types of crosshead guides have been used, reflecting the introduction of different wheel arrangements combined with a gradual increase in piston thrust.

In *A History of the American Locomotive,* John H. White Jr., wrote that one-, two- and four-bar crosshead guides were the most commonly used varieties during the mid-19th century. The predominance of 4-4-0 and 4-6-0 locomotives at that time resulted in the four-bar type being the most prevalent kind, because this guide arrangement was well suited to provide necessary clearance for the rear wheels of the leading truck. As locomotives grew more powerful, the traditional four-bar crosshead guides were no longer strong enough to provide adequate support for locomotives with much greater piston thrust. During the 1870s new types of stronger crosshead guides were developed.

One of the most common and recognizable two-bar crosshead arrangements is the so-called "alligator pattern" that uses bars of equal strength mounted above and below a symmetrically arranged crosshead. In theory, this arrangement allowed the crosshead's top and bottom bearing shoes to function interchangeably. However, in practice this was rarely the case because greater stress is placed on the top of the crosshead guide when the locomotive is running forward, and logically the stress is greater on the bottom guide when in reverse. Since most engines spend more time running forward than backward, the top guides tended to wear faster.

Forney explains that when the engine is working in forward gear "the backward stroke of the piston [puts] the strain on the [main rod which] tends to push the crosshead upward, and the forward part of the stroke . . .the [main rod] pulls the

The running gear on the fireman's side of Strasburg Railroad 2-6-0 no. 89 offers a good example of the alligator-style two-bar crosshead and cross-head guides. The cross-head keeps the piston in precise alignment inside the cylinder while transferring its thrust to the main rod, which constantly changes its angle at its connection to the crankpin. This locomotive's main rod is coupled to the second set of drivers, a common arrangement on late-era 2-6-0s. *Brian Solomon*

Alligator-style crosshead guides are characterized by equal guides above and below the crosshead (the piston rod is at full extension). This style was typical of late-era locomotives with high piston thrusts. *Russell Lee, Library of Congress*

crosshead in the same direction. If the crank turns the opposite way, this action is reversed and the crosshead would then be alternately pushed and pulled downward, and the bottom guides would be worn the most."

The result of this common wear pattern was that the respective characteristics of top and bottom bearing surfaces change relatively quickly in relation to one another. Despite this propensity for uneven wear, the alligator-style crosshead remained a common type until the end of steam and was especially popular on late-era switchers.

Another common crosshead type introduced in the late nineteenth century was the asymmetric arrangement developed by Pennsylvania Railroad master mechanic John P. Laird. This featured a suspended two-bar arrangement where the crosshead enclosed the lower guide bar while its top served as the bearing surface for the top guide bar. The top bar was the heavier member of the two guide bars.

In the 1900s, stronger crosshead types evolved. A multiple-bearing variety was introduced by the Pennsylvania Railroad circa 1915, which used a multiple grooved surface in a top-oriented guide as means to provide additional bearing surface and thus greater strength. This type was used on many of the most powerful late-era locomotives.

Main and side rods

The main rod connects the crosshead with the main driving wheel. With inside-connected engines, the main rod is located inside the locomotive frame and drives a cranked axle. On outside-connected locomotives (most after the mid-1800s) the rods are located outside the frames and connected using a crankpin on the primary driving wheel. Primary driver position relative to the other drivers varied depending on the design of the locomotive and the number of driving axles. Side rods are horizontal, and they transmit motion from the main driving wheel to the additional drivers.

A late-era evolutionary advancement was the extended main rod; essentially an intermediate side rod placed on the plane of the main rod aimed at reducing the load placed on the main crankpin by absorbing some of the piston thrust.

The degree of force placed on rods determined their size, shape, and relative flexibility. Early locomotives tended to use rounded rods. As power and piston travel increased, stronger rods were required, but it was also necessary to keep the reciprocating weight to a minimum. As a result, flat rods became standard. By the late 19th century even larger fluted-profile rods were adopted and became the common type on heavy 20th century engines.

A chief operating limitation for steam locomotives at higher speeds was the damaging centrifugal forces of the locomotive's reciprocating parts, a condition described as "dynamic augment"—the effects of forces that pound the locomotive and the tracks it runs on. These centrifugal forces increase significantly at higher speeds. Late-era designs combined improved materials and better counter-balancing techniques to minimize dynamic augment.

Metallurgical advances by the 1900s made possible lightweight-alloy steels that could be used for lighter and significantly stronger rods. Lighter, stronger rods, combined with precision counterweight techniques, were key elements of very capable high-speed locomotive designs. A Timken ad of the period bragged that one of its lightweight-alloy main rods weighed just 529 pounds compared to 1,003 pounds for a conventional rod.

The fastest of these modern locomotives included Milwaukee Road's famous streamlined 4-4-2 Atlantic types, built by Alco in 1935 for the railroad's briskly scheduled express *Hiawatha* services between Chicago, Milwaukee, and the Twin Cities, where engines worked at speeds in

The piston rod and crosshead on East Broad Top 15, a Baldwin-built narrow gauge 2-8-2, provides an example of the common Laird type two-bar crosshead guide that was widely used after about 1880. The crosshead enclosed the lower guide bar while the top bar contacted the crosshead's top facing surface. Also notice the crosshead connections for the valve gear, necessary to obtain the motion of the gear. *Brian Solomon*

The heavy main rod of Milwaukee Road S-3 4-8-4 no. 261 runs from the suspended-style crosshead at right to the main crank on the main driving wheel (the second driver). The locomotive, built by Alco in 1944, has 26 x 32-inch cylinders, 74" Boxpok drivers, and a top speed of 80 mph. *George W. Kowanski*

excess of 100 miles per hour. These featured state-of-the-art modern lightweight tandem main rods forged in an I-section profile from high-tensile-strength nickel-steel alloys.

Railway Mechanical Engineer profiled Milwaukee's new engines in 1935, explaining that "the counterbalancing of the locomotive is such that the dynamic augment at the rail at a speed of 100 mph is 10,800 pounds. The total reciprocating weights on one side of the locomotive amount to 1,003 pounds, of which one third are balanced. The low dynamic augment is due in part to the care in design to keep the weights of reciprocating parts as low as possible and also to the greatly reduced

This view of the main driving wheel, main crank, and side rod ends on Rio Grande 2-8-0 no. 346 shows an example of a forked-end side rod (also called a connecting rod), which is necessary to better distribute the piston thrust between the driving rods. *Brian Solomon*

overhang of the pin-borne weights due to the relatively narrow cylinder spread."

These late-era Atlantics featured main rods that were connected to the forward driving wheels, rather than the rear drivers as with most earlier Atlantic types. In another example of late-era design, Lima's pioneering H-10 Mikado, a precursor of the Super-Power 2-8-4 type, was among advanced locomotive designs that employed recently developed high-tensile alloy steel for reciprocating parts. The H-10's side rods and main rods were forged from heat-treated chrome-vanadium steel.

Wheels

The driving wheels (drivers) are the tallest wheels on the locomotive. They support the main weight of the locomotive and—through the main and side rods—power the locomotive. By the late 1800s, locomotives with four, six, and eight drivers were common; some later locomotives were built with 10 and 12 drivers.

Locomotives with low (small-diameter) driving wheels provide more tractive effort and power at slow speeds, but their top speed is limited. Those with tall drivers have less tractive effort but are more efficient, provide a better ride, and can travel at faster speeds. Driver diameter ranged from around 50" for switchers and slow freight locomotives to 60"-70" for fast freight locomotives to 80" for passenger locomotives.

To understand this, visualize the distance a locomotive can travel in one rotation (one power stroke each way for each cylinder) of the drivers. For a 50" driver, one revolution propels an engine 157" (13'-1"); an 80" driver nets a significantly longer distance: 251" (20'-11"). A rule of thumb is that a locomotive's top speed is roughly its driver diameter in miles per hour. This is the key factor in why steam locomotives were built for specific jobs, and why there were so many different combinations of wheel arrangements and wheel sizes.

Driving wheels have crankpins, to which the main and side rods attach, and to which the rods impart motion to the wheels. The main driving wheel (the one to which the

Opposite top: **Note how the main crank pin (on the main driving wheel, attached to the main rod) is heavier than the crank pins on the other drivers. Also note that the side rod between the main and third drivers is slightly heavier than the one between the third and fourth drivers, and the counterweight is larger on the main driver because of the additional rod weight.** *Robert Hale*

Opposite bottom: **The size and shape of locomotive rods can be seen here. These are fluted, with a ridge around the outside and depressed in the middle, giving them strength with less weight than a solid rod. The Santa Fe worker is magnafluxing the rods—sprinkling them with magnetic powder and then passing a magnetic cable loop over the rods—to check for defects.** *Wallace W. Abbey*

2

M.C.R.R.
NEW YORK CENTRAL LINES
8000

main rod is attached) has the main crankpin, which is heavier than crankpins on the other drivers. The crankpins on all drivers of a locomotive are located the same distance from the wheel center. This distance is set by the piston stroke: The crankpin on a turning wheel describes a circle with a diameter equal to the piston stroke.

Pilot wheels are small-diameter (typically 30" to 36" diameter) unpowered wheels at the front of a locomotive, usually as either a two- or four-wheel truck. These trucks usually have inbound-mounted journals, which help the wheels clear the cylinders. Pilot trucks' main purpose is stability, especially in helping guide the locomotive into and around curves at speed. Trailing wheels serve the same purpose when a locomotive is traveling in reverse. As locomotives became bigger and fireboxes expanded (and moved from above the drivers to behind the drivers) in the 1900s, two- and four-wheel trailing trucks supported the weight of the firebox and rear of the locomotive. Trailing wheels are often larger than pilot wheels, typically ranging from 36" to 48" in diameter.

Wheels on early steam locomotives used a variety of materials. Since railway vehicles were an outgrowth of stagecoach design, many early locomotives used wheels that bore a natural similarity to stage wheels. The first locomotives' wheels were made of a cast iron hub with wooden spokes, a wooden rim, and a thin outer rim consisting of a wrought iron tire. Examples included Stephenson's pioneering *Rocket* and many of the earliest American-built locomotives.

The rigors of railway service and the rapid growth in weight and size of locomotives soon made wooden wheel construction impractical, so more substantial

Opposite: Milwaukee Road's 4-4-2 Atlantics, built for fast *Hiawatha* passenger service, were among the fastest modern steam locomotives. Built in the mid-1930s by Alco, the 4-4-2s could top 100 mph on their runs. *Milwaukee Road*

New York Central (Michigan Central) 2-8-2 no. 8000 was a harbinger of the Super-Power era, with a bigger firebox, larger grate, improved superheater, and more flue capacity than earlier engines of similar size, giving it more power. It also used heat-treated chrome-vanadium steel for its main and side rods. *Lima*

On New York, Ontario & Western, the low (57") drivers of its 2-10-2 Santa Fe types gave them a lot of tractive effort for heavy freight service, but limited their top speed. Built in 1915, they were known as "Bull Mooses" on the railroad. *Brian Solomon collection*

materials were adopted. Yet, to the present day it is common among railroaders to refer to a poorly managed line or company starved for resources as a "wooden-axle outfit."

In *A History of the American Locomotive*, John H. White Jr. wrote that by the 1850s cast-iron drive wheels were standard and that the importance of locomotive wheels demanded special attention from manufacturers. These castings were made from high-quality materials with special emphasis on the cooling of components. Driving wheels continued to use a hub-spoke-rim design, while solid wheels were adopted for most unpowered leading and trailing wheels.

Owing to the high cost of driving wheels and rapid wear rates on the outside running surface, most locomotives used driving wheels with separate tires. These could be replaced as needed to prolong the life of the driving wheel. Cast iron was initially the preferred metal for locomotive tires, but the superior wearing characteristics of steel saw this material adopted for tires by the mid-1800s. Many railroads adopted steel for locomotive tires long before this metal was readily accepted for use in other components.

Railroads with tight curves and/or steep grades needed to replace tires more often than tangent flatland lines. Replacing locomotive tires was a routine but labor-intensive procedure. In the locomotive shop, the tire was heated, which caused the metal to expand, and then gradually forced off the wheel. In *Catechism of the Locomotive*, Forney describes fastening a locomotive tire: "The inside of the tires are usually turned out somewhat smaller than the outside of the wheel center. The tire is

The radial trailing truck was a significant innovation of the 1890s that contributed to the evolution of larger fireboxes and the introduction of several new locomotive types. This one has outside bearings (note the journal boxes); inside-bearing trucks are apparent by their exposed wheel faces. This is Reading & Northern 4-6-2 Pacific no. 425. *Brian Solomon*

Central Pacific's *CP Huntington* is a perfectly restored museum piece displayed at the California State Railroad Museum in Sacramento. Built by Danforth, Cooke & Company in 1863, the locomotive is named after Collis Porter Huntington, one of the railroad's founders. Note the ornamented driver with thin-profile spokes and the lightweight main rod (it only has two drivers; it has a 4-2-4 wheel arrangement). *Brian Solomon*

then heated so that it will expand enough to go on the center. It is then cooled off, and the contraction of the metal binds it firmly around the cast iron part of the wheel." In addition, fasteners called "security bolts" could be screwed through the wheel rim into the tire to prevent it from slipping off in the event that it got loose from the wheel.

Traditionally, driving wheels retained the common hub-and-spoke design. The shape and width of the spokes evolved over the years and necessarily grew heavier and more rugged as locomotives became larger and more powerful. The traditional T-profile spoke used in the formative years gave way to an oval shaped profile.

24
831
UNION PACIFIC

Changing a locomotive tire involves heating it until it expands and can be slipped off of the wheel. This is being done in the Duluth & Northeastern shops with a gas pipe placed around the tire and lighted (the feed pipe is visible at bottom. *John Gruber*

Another key component of each drive wheel is the counterweight, positioned 180 degrees opposite the crankpin to minimize the effect of damaging reciprocating forces from drive rods and pistons. As mentioned earlier, this force is significant, with individual rods sometimes weighing a thousand pounds or more. If not balanced properly, when a locomotive is at speed, these weights create a pounding motion on the track and also affect the locomotive, causing side-to-side motion (because the rods on either side are not aligned—they are quartered, or 90 degrees from each other). These forces become more severe as speed increases.

In the 1800s, techniques for calculating the amount of counter-balance were imperfect and limited the effectiveness of counterweights. More scientific approaches regarding counter-balancing were developed after World War I. Precision counter-balancing and cross-balance contributed to advanced wheel designs that minimized the effects of dynamic augment on the rail, and thus enabled sustained fast running with minimal damage to tracks and machinery. This advance contributed to the design of large high-speed steam locomotives such as modern 4-6-4s and 4-8-4s.

A disadvantage of the traditional rim-and-spoke wheel was a tendency over time for the rim to flatten out between spoke supports. Some improved late-era designs altered or abandoned the conventional formats and introduced new types of lightweight drivers that aimed at improving performance for heavy freight locomotives as well as passenger engines with large-diameter wheels.

The most-common of the new style of driving wheels was the Boxpok Driving Wheel Center (pronounced "box-spoke"; the name was a contraction of "box section-spoke") manufactured by General Steel Castings. An advertisement in the 1938 *Locomotive Cyclopedia* touted the advantages of the Boxpok wheel as being stronger, both laterally and in the rim section, with a design that prevents out-of-round wheels and flat spots, with greater resistance to lateral forces and rail impacts, all of which increase tire mileage and reduce wheel maintenance.

The Boxpok is actually hollow (like a "box") with internal reinforcements. It can

Opposite top: Union Pacific's later 4-8-4s were exceptional examples of the Northern type. Their 80"-diameter Boxpok driving wheels allowed speeds to 90 mph for fast freight or passenger service. Other late-era refinements included lightweight rods, multiple-ledge (multiple bearing surface) crossheads and guides, and boilers with a 300-pound operating pressure. *Robert A. Witbeck, collection of the Center for Railroad Photography & Art*

Opposite bottom: Iron locomotive tires predated the automotive-era rubber variety by more than a half century. Spare locomotive tires line the wall of East Broad Top's shops at Rockhill Furnace, Pa. Drive wheels are expensive, so railroads extended wheel life by using removable iron or steel tires on the primary wearing surface. *Brian Solomon*

Strasburg no. 89 is a 2-6-0 built in 1919 by the Canadian Locomotive Company for Grand Trunk Railway. This view shows its 63" driving wheels. Note that the main driver's counterweight is 180 degrees opposite the position of the crank pin. *Brian Solomon*

Reading class T-1 4-8-4 no. 2100 is equipped with Boxpok driving wheels. These feature box-section spokes and wheel rims in place of conventional spokes, allowing for better counterbalance to reduce the effects of dynamic augment at the rail. Note the tapered rod. *Chris Bost*

be spotted by its oval-shaped openings, which have smooth transitions (no lips or raised edges). The original Type A design had larger but fewer openings; the later Type B wheels had smaller but more openings.

Baldwin developed its own modern drive wheel design that it called the Baldwin Disc Wheel, which according to a period advertisement was cast from high-tensile steel using a pattern that featured a single arched disc section. This was merged with hollow triangular sections at the rim and hub that aimed at providing uniform support to all points of the rim. Baldwin boasted that this reduced dynamic augment by as much as 75 percent. They can be spotted by their oval (or "egg-shaped") openings with raised edges around the driver, with the face of the wheel inset between the holes.

Baldwin Disc Wheels have oval ("egg")-shaped openings with ridges, and a depressed area on the driver face around the wheel between the openings. These are on a Pennsylvania Railroad 4-4-4-4 equipped with oscillating valve gear. *Trains magazine collection*

This 72" General Steel Castings cast-steel Boxpok driver is for Santa Fe's class 3751 4-8-4 locomotive (the counterweight, crank pin, and tire have yet to be added). Compared to conventional spoke wheels, the Boxpok was a much stronger design and could better withstand the effects of high piston thrust. *General Steel Castings*

The Scullin Double Disc wheel center was another late-era type (introduced in 1932). These lightweight wheels were manufactured by the Scullin Steel Company from advanced steel alloys, and can be spotted by their plain appearance with small round holes in the wheel face. They were most-famously applied to some of New York Central's streamlined J3A Hudsons and were specially designed for improved appearance as well as superior performance. In 1939, Charles Shearer made famous the J3A's wheels with his detailed photographs and a world-famous painting titled *Rolling Power*.

Scullin promoted its design by pointing out that it provided better counterbalancing and permitted "the balancing of an increased amount of revolving and reciprocating weights." Also, "auxiliary counterbalance pockets are provided to ensure exact balancing, resulting in uniform performance of the drivers. The projection of the disc through the counter-balance on large-diameter centers eliminates an

look like Baldwin's design at first glance, but the openings are triangular with rounded corners and lack the depressed area on the wheel face of the Baldwin wheels. These are on Santa Fe 4-6-2 no. 3420; the railroad rebuilt the locomotive with Universal wheels. *Santa Fe*

Suspension is an important part of locomotive design, accomplished with a system of equalizers and springs on the frame behind the driving wheels. This view shows a heavy leaf spring above and behind the rear driving wheel on a 2-8-2 Mikado. *Brian Solomon*

eccentric condition at counterbalance location." The novelty of this type of wheel was in essence a spoke-less design.

The rarest of disk drivers were Universal driving wheels, made by Locomotive Furnished Metals. They have triangular openings around the driver face (with rims or ridges on the edges of the openings), but lack the inset feature of the similar Baldwin design. They were primarily used by Santa Fe as replacement drivers on rebuilt locomotives starting in the mid-1930s.

Suspension

Locomotives have rigid frames, but the axles are not mounted rigidly to the frame. As with an auto or truck, some form of springing and suspension is needed to cushion the ride and allow the wheels to move independently upward and downward as they negotiate rail joints, diamond crossings, and high and low points and other imperfections along the rails.

A system of levers (equalizers) and fulcrums interconnect the wheels on each side of the locomotive. They interact so that if one wheel raises, the neighboring wheels are pressed downward (see the drawing on page 117). Leaf springs at each wheel (at the fulcrum points) provide cushioning. A transverse equalizer connects the two sides.

These components are largely out of sight on a locomotive, located on the frame behind the drivers, although you can usually see the leaf springs behind the wheels. The photo on page 31 in chapter 1 has these components visible with the locomotive hoisted above the wheels.

Suspensions must also allow for lateral (side-to-side) movement of drivers as they negotiate curves and turnouts. Long-wheelbase locomotives (four or more sets of drivers) can be especially troublesome on sharp curves and turnouts. To aid with this, some long-wheelbase locomotives have flangeless driving wheels (known as "blind drivers" on a middle set of drivers.

Bearings

Bearings are critical load-carrying components designed to support rotating parts such as axles, rods, and crankpins. The tremendous weights involved, coupled with the speed of rotation of the moving parts and the small bearing surfaces, result in a great deal of friction force on the bearing surfaces. They require special attention and lubrication to keep them from scoring, seizing, or overheating.

On steam locomotives, bearings include those used for driving axles (known as main journal bearings), in journal boxes for leading and trailing axles, and those on rods and crank pins. In traditional locomotive practice, wheel and rod bearings comprised metal

Scullin double disc wheels are rather plain, with a series of round openings around the driver. New York Central was the primary user; this is on a streamlined J3a Hudson (4-6-4) with roller-bearing side rods. *New York Central*

blocks (or bushings) that were supported by or encased in a journal that could be filled with grease or oil. Typically, bearings were made from copper alloys with brass bearings—colloquially known as "brasses"—among the most common varieties.

An alternative to brass bearings were Babbitt metal bearings, named for their inventor, Isaac Babbitt. These were primarily tin with a minor amount of copper; they have a whitish alloy appearance, so were sometimes described as "white-metal bearings." A formula for Babbitt metal listed in the 1922 *Locomotive Cyclopedia* called for nine parts tin to one part copper.

All of these brass and white-metal bearings are considered "solid bearings" (sometimes incorrectly called "friction bearings"), distinguishing them from more modern roller bearings (more on those in a bit).

In *Catechism of the Locomotive,* Forney desribes main rod and side rod bearings: "The ends of the rods are provided with

Steam locomotive frames are rigid, but some type of suspension is needed to absorb shocks. The cylinders are cast at the front of the frame (left). Four driver sets will be added; the extension at right will support the firebox and ride atop the trailing truck. *Trains magazine collection*

Locomotive suspension

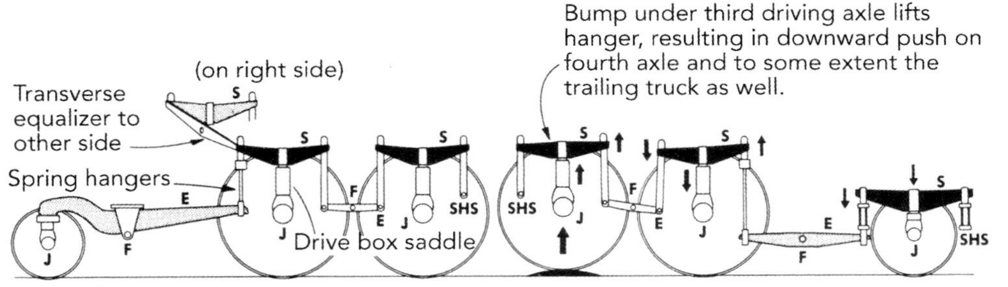

Key:
J — Journal bearings of wheels
S — Springs
E — Equalizers
F — Equalizer fulcrums (fixed to frame not shown)
SHS — Spring-hanger seats (also fixed to frame)

(Example at left is from a Georgia Northern 2-8-2)

A crew member checks the bearings on former Great Western Railway 2-10-0 no. 90 at the Strasburg Railroad. A traditional method of inspecting bearings is placing the back of a hand near the outside of the bearing to see if radiates heat. An overheated bearing can reach the melting point of metal, so crews avoid physical contact with bearing surfaces. *Brian Solomon*

what are called brass-bearings, brasses … These brasses are made in pairs, so as to embrace the pins, from each side. They are held by U-shaped clamps … called straps, which are bolted to the rods. When the brass-bearings become worn, they are taken out of the straps, and a portion of their surfaces of contact with each other is filed away, thus allowing them to come … together, and thereby reducing the size of the hole which receives the pin or journal. In order to prevent their being loose in the straps, tapered or wedge-shaped keys … which bear against the brasses, are fitted in the straps and rods. By driving down these keys the brass bearings are forced together, thus reducing the size of the hole for the journal, and making the rods the size of the hole for the journal, and making the rods fit tightly on the pins." By the early 20th century, his description would have seemed primitive, since as locomotives grew larger and their construction more sophisticated, the size, shape, and application of locomotive bearings evolved.

Solid bearings are high-wear components that require constant lubrication, regular inspection, and frequent replacement. An inadequately lubricated bearing is likely to overheat, and if a locomotive suffers a bearing failure working at speed it could have very serious consequences. At minimum the locomotive might be disabled, and in more serious situations an unattended bearing failure could result in a broken axle or rod, derailment, and injuries to the locomotive crew. This is why whenever possible, typically during prolonged station stops, water and fuel stops, or at meeting points, a member of the engine crew would check bearings for signs of excessive heat and adequate lubrication.

Roller bearings

Roller bearings were a post-World War I innovation that eventually revolutionized

Santa Fe shop worker John Mohn applies a lube gun to grease the rods on Pacific no. 3427. This lubricator used 130 pounds of pressure to do the job, and it typically required 20 minutes to finish one locomotive. The 4-6-2 has been rebuilt with Universal disk driving wheels, a rare style distinguished by triangular openings outlined by a ridge. *Santa Fe*

many areas of railroading. Although some steam locomotives took advantage of their benefits, roller bearings' widespread adoption came after most steam had been retired.

The basic roller bearing is a sealed assembly comprising four groups of parts: an outer ring ("race"), an inner race, and a separator ("cage"); positioned between the inner and outer races are the rollers from which the bearing takes its name. Roller bearings come in a variety of circular shapes, but the most common for railroad applications is a solid tapered cylinder. The roller bearing assembly is a tightly manufactured component. It is made from high-quality, high-carbon alloy steels (typically including chromium, nickel and/or other hard metals.)

Unlike traditional brass bearings that were heavily dependent on lubrication to minimize friction between two surfaces moving against each other, a roller bearing uses the highly polished finish and hardness of the multiple roller surfaces in the bearing. While lubrication is still crucial for roller bearings, it's within a sealed package. Roller bearings provide less rolling resistance, have significantly longer life, and are far less likely to suffer a failure than a solid bearing during the normal course of operation.

The railroad industry, however, was traditionally distrustful of new technology—especially when it came with a significantly higher initial price tag. Thus, despite the promise of lower friction, higher reliability, and lower maintenance, railroads were reluctant to embrace roller bearings. By the late 1920s, roller bearings had proven successful for use on passenger cars and tender trucks, and yet railroads still thought they were too fragile for punishing service as primary locomotive bearings.

Knowing that the railroads were a hard sell, the Timken Company (among the primary American manufacturers of roller

Union Pacific rebuilt 4-8-2 no. 7002 with roller bearings and new Timken rods and components in 1936, then added streamlining to it in 1937. The railroad reported it cost $16,308 to add roller bearings. The locomotive was used as backup power for passenger trains, but the shrouding was removed in 1942. *Timken*

To demonstrate the virtues of roller bearings, in 1930 Timken commissioned Alco to build 4-8-4 no. 1111 with roller-bearing journals on axles and rod connections. It was known by its nickname Four Aces and featured card suit symbols—spade, heart, diamond, club—in its number boards. It's shown just prior to embarking on its 21-month demonstration tour of the U.S. *Trains magazine collection*

This publicity photo shows three men pulling Timken no. 1111 (which weighed 355 tons) on level track. This was distributed to the press with the caption, "Timken roller bearings on all axles practically eliminates all resistance to motion." *Timken*

bearings) made a bold move in 1930 and ordered its own custom-built locomotive specially fitted with roller bearings in a bid to convince the reluctant railroad industry of the benefits afforded by Timken roller bearings.

Timken worked with Alco in the design of a state-of-the-art 4-8-4 based largely on a New York Central design. It was intended to accommodate clearances on virtually all American main lines to facilitate demonstration runs around the country. To help defray construction costs, Timken partnered with 52 individual parts suppliers to contribute to the engine, while defraying billing until after the locomotive had completed its tests and demonstrations and could be sold.

Timken's locomotive was known as the Four Aces, no. 1111, with playing card

Solid bearings were a constant source of trouble for locomotives and rolling stock alike. When a bearing overheats, it requires immediate attention or catastrophic bearing or axle failure can result. Here a trainman attends to an overheated bearing on a narrow-gauge freight car on Denver & Rio Grande Western's San Juan extension. *John Gruber, collection of the Center for Railroad Photography & Art*

The engineers of both locomotives of a double-headed Santa Fe passenger extra are taking advantage of a station stop at Kingman, Ariz., to oil their locomotives' valve gear and crossheads. The year is 1944 and the lead engine is Pacific 1306, built by Baldwin in 1911. *Jack Delano, Library of Congress*

symbols—heart, spade, diamond, and club—on its sandbox number boards. It was dressed in a conservative dark green with gold stripes with TIMKEN painted in bold serif letters on the tender. It was delivered in April 1930 and embarked on a 21-month tour of American railroads, working on both passenger and freight trains. To demonstrate the low friction of its bearings, Timken arranged a team of three young women to pull the engine with a rope before a line of eager reporters. More significantly, the Four Aces' bearings showed no appreciable signs of wear after 100,000 miles of service.

Roller bearings not only reduced the incidence of bearing failure, but importantly allowed locomotives greater starting power and required less lubrication and less maintenance. During the 1930s, roller bearings began to be adopted for many new locomotives' main axles. Less common were engines equipped with roller bearings on main and side rods as well as valve gear components.

Some progressive railroads such as Norfolk & Western made wide use of roller bearings on their late-era locomotive designs including its A, J, and Y Class engines. Other railroads took advantage of the technology by retrofitting older engines with roller bearings. However, the coming of diesels precluded widespread adaptation, and most steam locomotives continued to rely on old-school solid bearings until the end of their service in the 1940s and 1950s.

Now that we've learned how to put a locomotive into motion, the next chapter will examine how a locomotive stops—turn the page for a look at locomotive brakes and accessories.

Roller bearings are sealed units that rely on multiple hard-metal conical or cylindrical rollers to transfer motion. This cutaway view shows what's inside the assembly. *Hyatt*

Chapter 5

Air brakes

Union Pacific Big Boy no. 4019 drifts downgrade with a long freight on Wyoming's Sherman Hill. The haze of brake-shoe smoke along the train is a good indication that the brakes have been applied to check the train's downhill speed. *Robert A. Witbeck, collection of the Center for Railroad Photography & Art*

In the early years of railroading, the process of slowing or stopping a train was slow, clumsy, labor intensive, and dangerous. Into the 1870s, engineers relied upon primitive locomotive brakes and brakemen riding atop cars to set brakes manually using hand wheels. Brakemen rode the cars waiting for a signal from the engineer to set and release brakes.

This system was especially hazardous for the brakemen—particularly in mountainous and hilly territory—who had to ride the tops of cars in all weather and day and night. The inability to stop trains quickly hampered train operations, limiting train size to 15 to 20 cars and greatly limiting the speeds that trains could safely travel. Freights in particular were kept to a moderate pace, rarely exceeding 20 mph.

The invention of automatic air brakes in the latter part of the 19th century was one of the most important innovations for railroading. Railroads were initially distrustful of the air brake, and resisted its implementation because of the high cost of installing the equipment. It wasn't until the turn of the 20th century that most American trains benefited from continuous automatic brakes; by 1905, 2 million cars and 89,000 locomotives were so equipped.

The air brake was a key factor in steam locomotive development as well. Because the automatic brake allowed longer, heavier, faster trains, railroads and manufacturers responded by quickly developing larger locomotives with more power to handle these trains. This in turn led to innovations and advancements in locomotive design.

A trainman ties down a freight car's hand-brake with the aid of a wooden club. This view is reminiscent of the days before air brakes became standard equipment on all cars, when brakemen faced the perilous job of walking atop moving cars to set and release brakes by hand following whistle signals from the engineer. *John Gruber, collection of the Center for Railroad Photography & Art*

The Westinghouse Air Brake

George Westinghouse was the genius behind the air brake. In 1869 he demonstrated his original straight air brake, which used a system of piped compressed air to activate pneumatic cylinders that set brake shoes to grip railcar wheels throughout a train. In this system, an engine-driven air pump supplied compressed air to a main reservoir (tank). The engineer applied and released the brakes with a control stand that had three settings: running (no brakes applied; no air in train line), applying (air being admitted to train line from the reservoir), and holding (train line sealed to hold in air to keep brakes applied). (See the drawings on page 127.)

Although an improvement over having brakemen riding cars, the straight air system had several weaknesses. The brakes applied from front to back as air entered the train line, and it took several seconds for the brakes on each car to react. This could cause severe slack run-ins as cars in the rear rammed into forward cars that had begun

Westinghouse Air Brakes

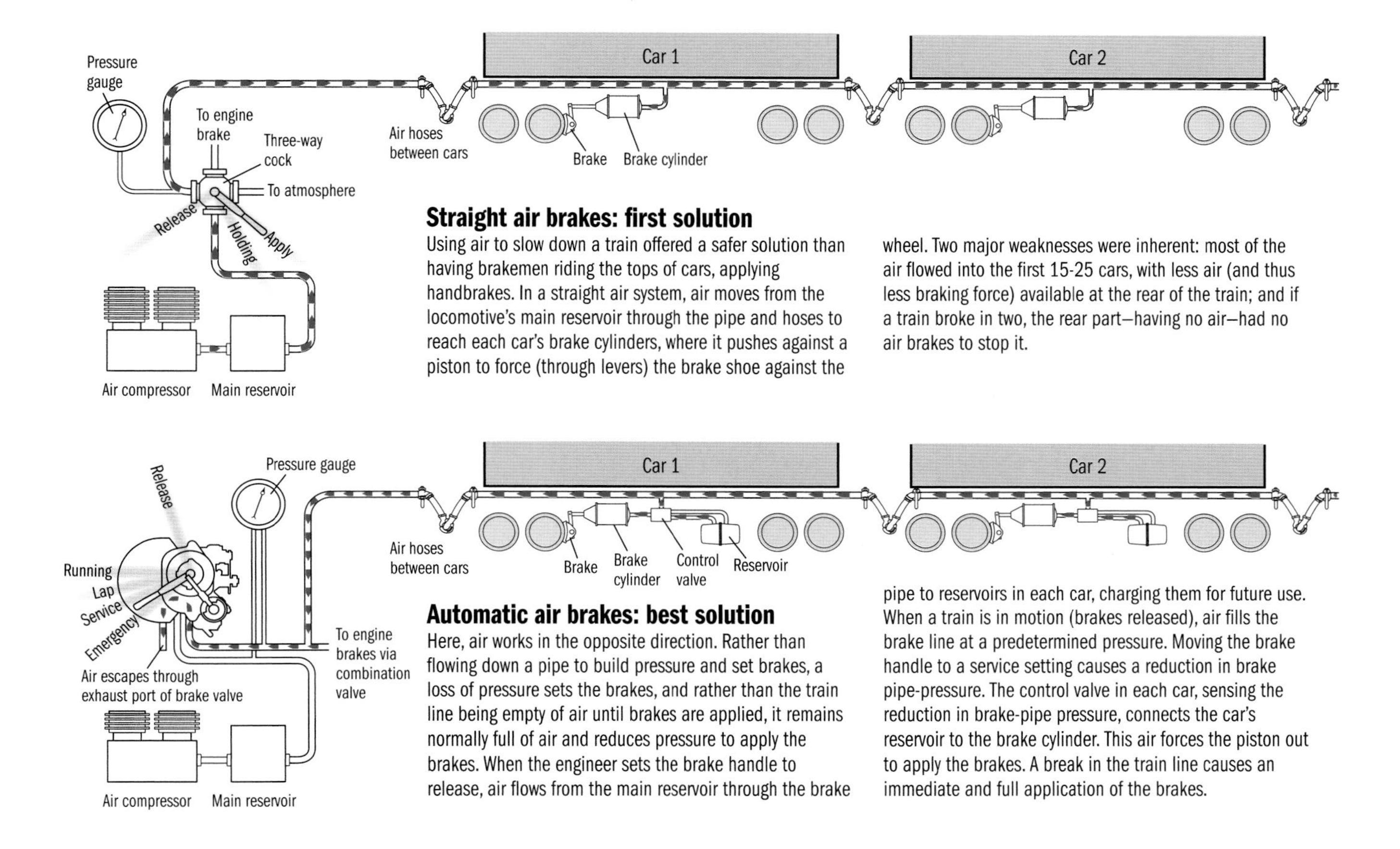

Straight air brakes: first solution

Using air to slow down a train offered a safer solution than having brakemen riding the tops of cars, applying handbrakes. In a straight air system, air moves from the locomotive's main reservoir through the pipe and hoses to reach each car's brake cylinders, where it pushes against a piston to force (through levers) the brake shoe against the wheel. Two major weaknesses were inherent: most of the air flowed into the first 15-25 cars, with less air (and thus less braking force) available at the rear of the train; and if a train broke in two, the rear part—having no air—had no air brakes to stop it.

Automatic air brakes: best solution

Here, air works in the opposite direction. Rather than flowing down a pipe to build pressure and set brakes, a loss of pressure sets the brakes, and rather than the train line being empty of air until brakes are applied, it remains normally full of air and reduces pressure to apply the brakes. When the engineer sets the brake handle to release, air flows from the main reservoir through the brake pipe to reservoirs in each car, charging them for future use. When a train is in motion (brakes released), air fills the brake line at a predetermined pressure. Moving the brake handle to a service setting causes a reduction in brake pipe-pressure. The control valve in each car, sensing the reduction in brake-pipe pressure, connects the car's reservoir to the brake cylinder. This air forces the piston out to apply the brakes. A break in the train line causes an immediate and full application of the brakes.

Similar brake rigging is used in straight and automatic air: the difference is in the valve.

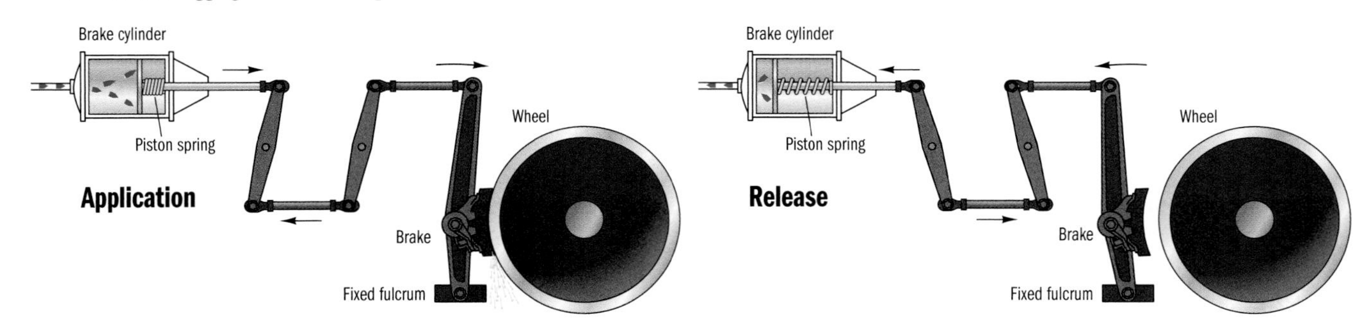

The locomotive engineer controls the working of the automatic air brake using cab-mounted brake valves such as this one (on Sierra Railroad no. 28). Operation of the valve is from left to right in a counterclockwise arc. At far left is the "release" position; at far right is the "emergency" position which evacuates all air from the train line and applies the brakes as quickly as possible. Individual controls are used for the train brake and independent (locomotive) brake.
Brian Solomon

slowing. This still limited top speeds and train size (to about 25 cars). Leaks in the train line and air hoses could cause brakes to gradually bleed off after being applied, especially on downgrades where the brakes had to remain applied for extended time. Straight air brakes also had a major flaw: Any leak or break along the supply line (broken air hose, accidental uncoupling, compressor failure) resulted in a complete loss of brakes.

In 1872, Westinghouse introduced his much-improved automatic air brake system. It is the forerunner of the system still in use today (although it has been considerably modified and improved). The new system was designed to be as fail-safe as possible, so in the event of a brake system failure the brakes would apply automatically and thus bring a train to a stop. Significantly, this system featured an air reservoir on each car, along with a triple valve on each car (a three-way control valve designed to charge the reservoirs and apply and release the brakes).

The key modification in the new system was that the train line (pipes running the length of the train, with air hoses connecting cars) was always charged with air. The triple valve on each car detects changes in train-line air-pressure to control brake functions using the car's air supply (reservoir), while recharging their cars' air reservoirs between brake applications. This greatly improved each car's response and braking time.

The brake valve in the locomotive cab still regulated the brakes, but with more control, by adjusting pressure changes in the train line. Reducing the pressure triggers the valves on each car to set brakes: the car's valve transfers air from the car's reservoir to the brake cylinder, which applies the brake shoes to the wheels. The engineer adjusts the strength of the brake application by the amount of air released from the train line. Recharging the train line (increasing pressure) signals the valve on each car to release its brakes, whereupon it begins recharging its car's reservoir from the train line.

The system's best feature was that it insured that any interruption that dropped brake-pipe pressure (such as a broken hose) automatically set the train brakes. Another advantage was that adding cars to a train didn't reduce the effectiveness of the air brake, as was the case with the straight air brake system.

Although it was in theory a fail-safe system, early automatic air brakes were far from flawless. While they provided a faster and more-reliable means of setting brakes—and greatly improved train handling—it took a degree of skill to keep a train under control. Setting and releasing the brake

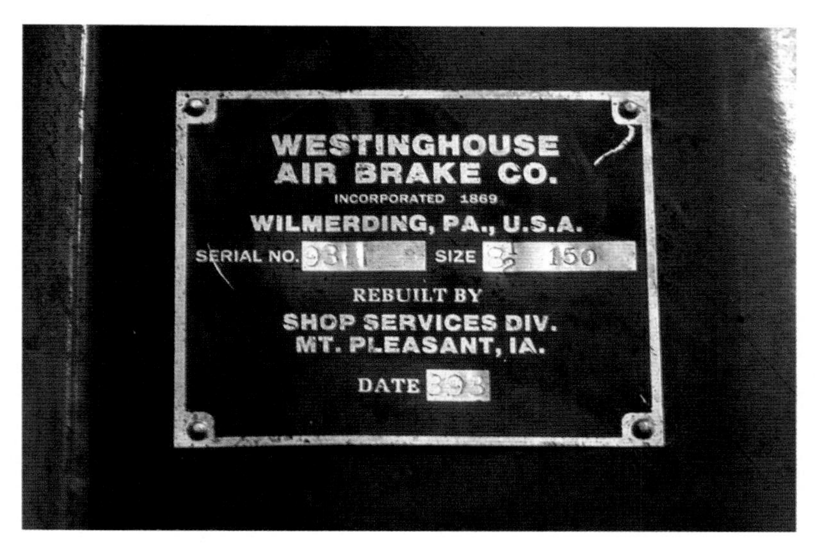

Top: George Westinghouse is the father of the air brake, and the company that bears his name built (and builds) system components, including this locomotive air pump on a Rio Grande narrow-gauge 2-8-2. The builder's plate shows it has an 8½" piston and pumps 150 cubic feet of air per minute. *Brian Solomon*

Above: The brakes have been applied on this Milwaukee Road locomotive, with the brake shoes firmly clamping to the wheel treads. *Milwaukee Road*

didn't happen instantly. The air pressure changes needed to work along the train line, which could lead to uneven braking action, especially on long trains or with a mix of cars of varying weights and lengths.

A further advancement to the system included introduction of the Westinghouse Quick Action Automatic Brake of 1888, which featured a much-improved variation of the triple valve with an emergency valve position. This was designed for the rapid release of air from the train line to set the brakes as quickly as possible.

Locomotives also had an "independent brake"—a separate system that only controls locomotive braking. This gives an engineer added train control because the locomotive brakes can be operated separately from the rest of the train.

Despite its advantages, the automatic air brake wasn't immediately universally adopted. Railroads balked at the expense, and it would take time to fit a million-plus cars with equipment. Air brakes were eventually implemented in stages over three decades. In 1889, new standards and rules were introduced for the interchange of cars equipped with automatic brakes. In 1893, the passage of the Railroad Safety Appliance Act finally mandated implementation of industry-wide, standardized automatic brakes for freight trains with a target date of 1900 (the Act included automatic couplers as well). In reality, it took several more years before air brakes were universal, and into the early 1900s railroad rulebooks still listed provisions for carrying freight cars without air brakes (specifying the percentage of cars in a train that must be equipped with brakes, and that cars without brakes be handled at the end of the train).

Air brakes in the 1900s

In *The Science of Railways,* published in 1903, author Marshall M. Kirkman offered this period description of how air brakes of the time worked. "The essential parts of the automatic brake system are the air gauge and pump governor; air pump and main reservoir; train line (brake pipe) with hose couplings and branch pipes; triple valve, auxiliary reservoir, and brake cylinder.

"The operation of the air through the automatic system is, briefly, as follows: The air pump takes air from the atmosphere and compresses it into the main reservoir; it then passes through the engineer's valve (in release position) to the train line. From the train line the air passes through the branch pipe, cut-out cock, and triple valve of each car into its auxiliary reservoir. When the brakes are to be set, a movement of the triple valve allows the air to pass from the auxiliary

Northern Pacific class D-3 2-6-0 no. 469, built by Baldwin in the 1890s, simmers by a coaling tower sometime around 1900. Like most early steam locomotives, it has one single-rod air compressor, located just in front of the cab. The main air reservoir is the large cylindrical tank positioned horizontally beneath the running board. *Brian Solomon collection*

[reservoir] to the brake cylinder, applying the brake. When the brake is to be released, the movement of the triple valve to its original position allows the air in the brake cylinder to escape into the atmosphere. When a retaining pressure valve is applied to a car, the triple [valve] exhaust is piped to the retainer, which must, of course, be open to allow the free escape of all air from the cylinder. The train pipe under each car is connected by its branch pipe to a triple valve. The latter derives its name from the fact that it performs three operations of charging the auxiliary reservoir, setting the brake, and releasing it; and, as each operation depends directly upon the triple valve, it become the most important feature of the automatic brake, and is perhaps, the most difficult of comprehension."

Kirkland explained that the triple valve had four connections: to the train line, the auxiliary reservoir, the brake cylinder, and an exhaust to the atmosphere. The movement of air (communication) between these connections is controlled by the valve as follows:

"To release the brake, communication is opened between the train line and auxiliary reservoir, closed between the auxiliary reservoir and the brake cylinder, and opened between the brake cylinder and the atmosphere. On the other hand, to set the brake, communication is closed between the train line and auxiliary reservoir, opened between the auxiliary reservoir and brake cylinder, and closed between brake cylinder and the atmosphere."

The system functions by reacting to changes in air pressure. "When the train line and all the auxiliary reservoirs of a train have a pressure of seventy pounds per square inch, they are said to be fully charged. The feed port in the triple valve is so small that about two minutes are required to charge an auxiliary, if seventy pounds pressure be maintained in the train line continually.

"The two pressures, train line and auxiliary reservoir, control the movements of the triple valve by the preponderence [sic] of the one over the other. The law governing the triple valve is as follows: the triple valve moves to set position when the train line pressure is reduced to less than that pressure in the auxiliary reservoir, and to release position when the train line pressure exceeds that in the auxiliary reservoir.

"Venting the auxiliary reservoir pressure to the atmosphere by the release valve, or 'bleeder,' is termed 'bleeding' a car. The brake releases through the triple valve as soon as the auxiliary reservoir pressure is less than that of the train line. The principle is precisely the same as when the engineer releases by increasing the train line above the auxiliary reservoir pressure."

The engineer's air-brake control valve is located in the cab. This control was subject to numerous improvements over the years. The F6 or "1892" valve described by Kirkman below in 1903, was the latest and most advanced brake control valve for the time. It offered far more control than the original straight-air controls, but it is primitive in comparison with those used in modern diesel-electric locomotives. Aiding an engineer's control of the brakes are gauges in the cab that show pressure in the main reservoir and train line. Further, the control valve's audible exhaust in the locomotive cab provided a feeling for how the brake was functioning.

The control valve operated with a handle that turns in the counter-clockwise direction and featured five positions: in order, release, running, lap, service application, and emergency.

Operation of the steam-era airbrake system required a series of steps that Kirkman detailed, with the five positions on the engineer's rotary valve handle being as follows:

1) Release (or "full release")—connects the main reservoir (on the locomotive) to the train line. This position is for quickly charging the train line and auxiliary (car) reservoirs, also for releasing brakes.

2) Running—a modification of release. Used when a train is moving and not requiring braking when the brakes have been released.

3) Lap—closes all ports in the engineer's valve. Used between brake applications, when a train has parted or the conductors's valve opened, and also when coupling to air-braked cars.

4) Service—used to set the brakes.

A trainman makes an adjustment to the single-rod air compressor on Central Railroad of New Jersey no. 113, an Alco-built 0-6-0 switcher. Notice the crosshead-actuated lubrication equipment to the right of the piston valve. *Pat Yough*

5) Emergency—opens the train line wide open to the atmosphere directly; results quickly in a full brake application.

Railroaders often describe an emergency action as "the big hole," as the action quickly dumps the air through what is in effect a large hole in the train line—stopping a train this way is "big-holing it" or "putting a train in the big hole." A train stopped after an emergency application is "in emergency."

Today's diesel engineers have the advantage of locomotive-based dynamic braking and advanced air-brake response times on cars; even with that, it takes a deft hand on the controls to safely and smoothly control train speed. This was even more the case of steam operations as train size increased dramatically from the 1910s into the 1920s. Even though the automatic brake is a good system with many built-in safeguards, it was still possible for trains to lose control and run away down grades. These challenges increase dramatically as train length (and thus train weight and brake response time) increases and as grades increase in steepness and length.

As motive-power expert Ed King wrote in the March 2004 issue of *Trains,* "it's not like driving a car; you can't just step on the brake at any time you feel like it and get results. The reservoirs only hold so much air, the brake pipe can feed it to the reservoir only so fast, and the air compressors on the locomotive can't run overtime."

A telltale sign of heavy brake applications in steam days was the low fog of brakeshoe smoke that hung low over a train, especially on long downhill grades. The brake shoes would heat the wheels to a point that spilled oil from journal boxes would begin to smoke, causing a sight (and smell) that old-time railroaders instantly recognize.

Locomotive components

To power the brakes, a reliable, high-volume air supply is critical for a locomotive. Not only did the air brakes work using air, accessories such as the automatic bell ringer and sanders also tapped into the air supply. Air compressors (air pumps) were prominent pieces of equipment on steam locomotives, and their size, number, type, and location varied by era, locomotive type, and railroad.

This wide-angle view shows a Westinghouse cross-compound air compressor on the left side of a Rio Grande class K36 narrow gauge 2-8-2. The back-and-forth piping at left cools the compressed air as it travels to the reservoir.
Brian Solomon

Westinghouse was the main supplier, but New York Air Brake was also a widely used source of components.

The first locomotives equipped for air brakes typically used a single-rod pump air compressor (with a 9½" or 11" piston), powered by steam, located on the right or left side of the firebox. These were also called single-cylinder or "one-lung" compressors. The air reservoir (tank) could be mounted within the locomotive frame or under the cab. After 1900, locomotives were fitted with two reservoirs. Because air becomes hot as it is compressed, the pipe from the compressor to the reservoir was quite long (usually at least 75 feet) to allow the air to cool before entering the reservoir. This pipe is often visible, and part of it is often in a back-and-forth pattern along the running board.

As locomotives increased in power and train size and speed increased, air pump capacity also increased. Some locomotives received a pair of single-rod compressors; more common was the use of a two-rod (cross-compound) compressor, which used a pair of pistons. These are tied together as one unit, so that the exhaust from the first cylinder is used to drive the second cylinder. By the late 1920s, many locomotives were being equipped with two cross-compound compressors—this was especially true for railroads operating in mountainous territory or those running long trains.

Typical modern air pump location was on the left side, just under the running board along the boiler. Many railroads located the pumps at the locomotive front, either mounted on the pilot deck or on the front of the smokebox. Air reservoirs were typically long cylinders mounted under the running boards.

The brake valves are located atop a control stand on the engineer's side of the cab, typically directly in front of the cab seat and below the throttle. Directly above that are gauges that show the air pressure in the reservoir and train line.

Locomotives have brake shoes that, when applied, contact the treads of the drivers. They operate in much the same way as the brakes on railroad cars.

Improvements

Once locomotives and rolling stock on the North American rail network were fully equipped with automatic air brakes, numerous improvements were made to brake controls, valves, and other components (on cars as well as locomotives), making the system faster responding and giving it a higher degree of safety and reliability. A major upgrade came with the AB brake system in 1930, which included separate components for the control valve (no longer a "triple valve"), reservoir (now including separate service and emergency sections), and cylinder. The AB system worked faster and was more reliable than the older K system, which had the triple valve attached to the reservoir (and the KC variation had the valve, reservoir, and cylinder all combined). The control valves likewise improved over the years, with improved sensitivity and response time.

Looking back, the transitional years of the early 1900s seem archaic when compared to the advancements in air brake systems, while the industry's formative years when trains operated without benefit of Westinghouse's automatic air brake system are beyond comprehension.

Chesapeake & Ohio 2-8-8-2 no. 1547 has a pair of cross-compound air pumps in front of the smokebox. The front of the locomotive is crowded, with an Elesco feedwater heater (at top), bell, class lights, and low-mounted headlight. The massive articulateds were colloquially known as "Simple Simons." This is at Newport News, Va., in 1939. *Richard E. Prince*

Locomotive accessories and components

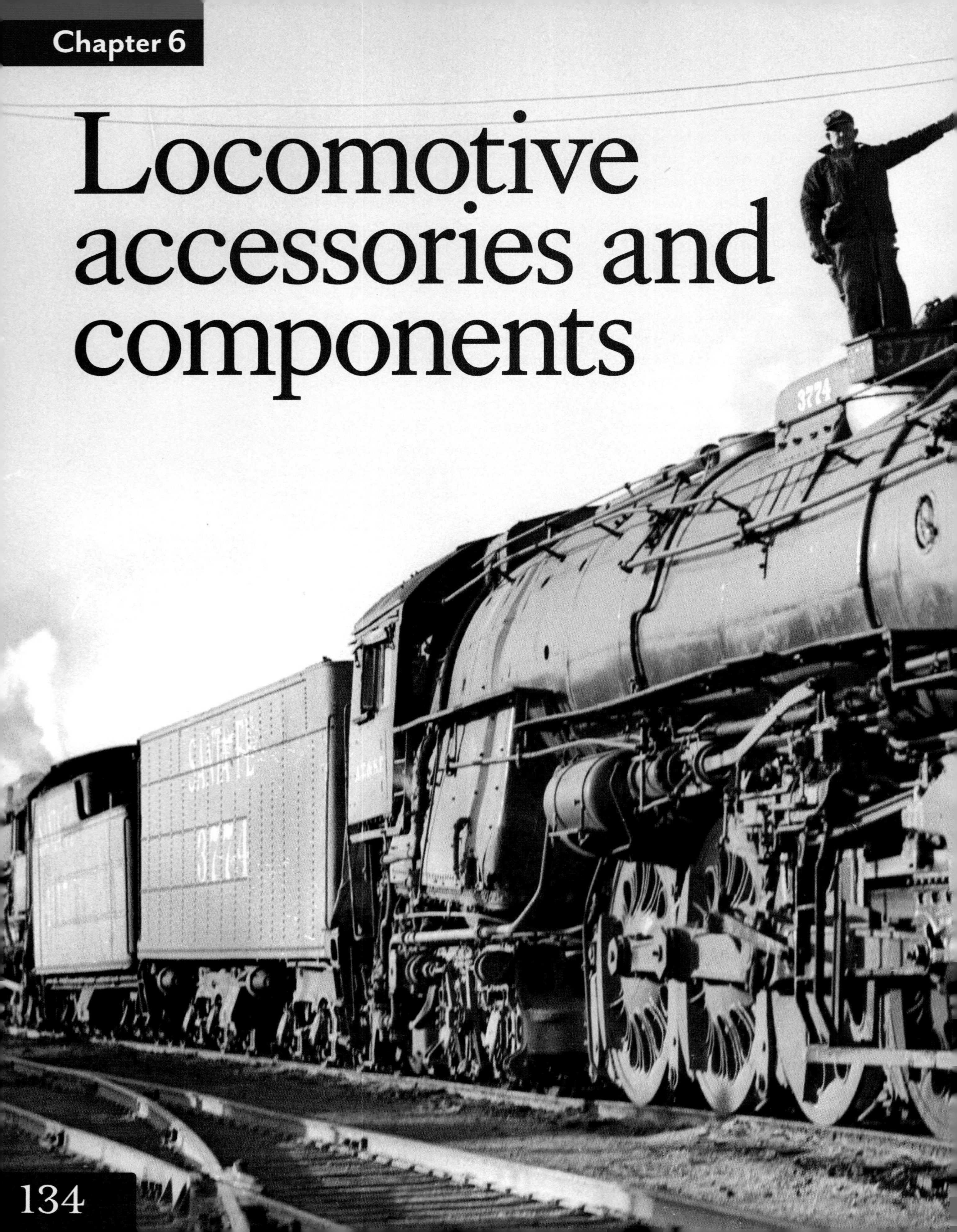

The fireman fills the sand box on Santa Fe 4-8-4 no. 3774 at Slaton, Texas, on Feb. 21, 1953. A number of locomotive appliances are visible in this photo: pneumatically operated bell atop the smokebox; headlight with number plate; class lights (at each corner above the smokebox front); boiler-tube pilot; and steps leading to stepped running board (with handrail running their length). *Robert A. Witbeck, collection of the Center for Railroad Photography & Art*

Along with all of the locomotive parts we've already discussed are number of additional locomotive components that contribute to safety, convenience, or operation. These include whistles, bells, headlights, classification lights, pilots, grab irons, lubricators, sand boxes, and other appliances. All evolved over time with their use varying by era and railroad.

Bells

One of the distinctive characteristics of North American locomotive operation is the clanging of the bell. This simple device is part of railroad culture and its correct use is governed by its earliest rules. The bell is used as a warning when an engine starts to move or when it crosses a highway at grade. The distant sound of a locomotive bell ringing in a yard on a foggy night or a cold winter's morning will sound a chord in memory that might last a lifetime.

In *A History of the American Locomotive,* John H. White traced the origins of the locomotive bell to Massachusetts legislation in 1835—a reaction to an accident on the Boston & Worcester a year earlier. From that early time it was required by Massachusetts state law that locomotives ring a bell when approaching crossings. The simplicity of the locomotive bell resulted in it becoming standard equipment.

Steam locomotive bells were typically fairly heavy. They were designed to be heard over the sounds of the locomotive exhaust and their sound had to carry a considerable distance. The typical early location was mounted atop the boiler, suspended in a wrought iron frame that allowed it to freely swing back and forth. Operation was manual, with the engineer starting the bell swinging by pulling on a cord in the cab.

By the 20th century, as locomotive operation grew more complex, many locomotives were equipped with automatic bell-ringing devices (usually air powered). This made ringing the bell easier—opening

Manually operated bells (note the pull cord extending back toward the cab) were usually mounted atop the boiler in front of the steam dome (at right). The device in the middle is a Sunbeam turbo-generator ("dynamo") for powering the headlight and other locomotive lights. Note the wisp of steam exhaust from the turbo-generator. *Pat Yough*

and closing a valve in the cab turned it on and off—and also facilitated more diverse bell placement, since a direct cord connection was no longer necessary. Bells could be located in front of the smokebox or below the running boards. One such mechanism, the Viloco Improved Gollman Bell Ringer, was powered by a small vertically oriented pneumatic cylinder controlled by its own throttle valve.

Railroad rule books specify when bells should be rung. Specific rules varied among railroads, but generally bells were rung when trains began moving and as a warning in other situations. As an example, Boston & Albany (the successor to bell-pioneer Boston & Worcester) rules in 1942 required the bell to be rung when an engine is about to move, when approaching a public crossing at grade, in emergencies, and at points where required by law or special instructions. These usually included locations such as public station platforms, areas where vision was obscured, and other areas where people typically congregated.

Whistles

No sound is as identifiable with the steam locomotive as the steam whistle. A British innovation, the steam whistle first appeared on locomotives in the 1830s. Whereas British whistles tended toward shrill, high-pitched tones, American locomotive whistles spanned a wide range of deeper, more-melodic sounds, and some of the most distinctive multi-tone whistles issued low soul-piercing chords.

Railroads used many types of whistles, but one of the most common arrangements used an inverted brass cup (sometimes described as a "bell"—not to be mistaken for the common locomotive bell as previously described). This was positioned tightly over an annular opening and designed to make a distinctive pitch when the edge of the cup was blasted with steam from the boiler. The overall shape was a vertical cylinder. Steam admission was controlled with a valve opened manually using a pull cord in the locomotive cab. The frequency of the tone is dependent on the proportions of the whistle-cup and the size of its opening(s). Skill and manipulation of the whistle valve allowed for infinite variations in sounds from individual locomotive whistles.

J.G.A. Meyer, author of the 1892

With a short blast, the whistle of Middletown & Hummelstown no. 91 could be heard resounding across the landscape. There's something stirring about a steam whistle that picks us up and carries us to another time. *Brian Solomon*

The whistle cord and lever are apparent in this view, with the dynamo at left. The safety valve is next to the whistle.
Pat Yough

book *Modern Locomotive Construction,* describes a chime whistle patented by the Crosby Steam Gauge and Valve Company of Boston: "The peculiar features of this whistle are found in the construction of the bell, which is divided into three compartments. One of these compartments extends throughout the whole length of the bell; the second compartment is made somewhat shorter, and the third still shorter. The whistle valve need not differ in construction from that of any other whistle, and can be made to suit the taste and experience of the designer. This whistle produces three distinct tones, which harmonize and give an agreeable musical chord; and when they are used on passenger trains exclusively, serve to distinguish the latter from freight trains. These whistles have been adopted for passenger service on several railroads, and are favorably endorsed."

Whistles are generally located atop the boiler, and are often mounted on the steam dome (often next to the safety/pressure-relief valve).

Over the years, whistles evolved from a warning device into an important part of railroad communication. In the days before portable radios, railroaders relied upon whistle signals as a means of conveying vital operating instructions. Whistle signals comprised sequences of long (shown as "—") and short ("o") blasts. Probably the best known is the "— — o —" as trains approach grade crossings. Others included

In the days before electric lights, headlights required a large parabolic reflector to amplify the dim light provided by an oil lamp. They were generally mounted on a platform above the smokebox. This is Milwaukee Road 4-4-0 no. 723. *Milwaukee Road*

signals for starting a train ("— —") and various indications for brakemen. Railroad rule books specified what each signal meant: See the chart on page 149 for several examples.

Whistles were also used as general warning signals, for example for people or vehicles on track or approaching areas where crews are working or vision might be obscured.

Headlights and markers

Early locomotive headlights were not electric lights, but instead were lanterns with a wick and flame to provide light. In the mid-nineteenth century a common type of headlight was a large metal enclosure called an Argand burner that was positioned on a bracket on the front of the smokebox. Headlight placement varied from railroad to railroad, but most lines preferred high-mounted headlights near the top of the boiler for best visibility. The Argand burner was designed with a hollow cylindrical wick to facilitate rapid combustion and therefore supply greater than normal air current to provide a brighter flame. The lamp was positioned in front of a specially designed concave parabolic reflector, typically made from copper and silver-plated metal, that directed light into a parallel light beam ahead of the locomotive.

Among operating crew responsibilities was headlight maintenance. Oil needed to be checked and filled, and the reflector required regular polishing. The lamp wick had to be trimmed before lighting. Headlights were only lit at night, as during the day they would be virtually invisible. By modern standards these old headlights were quite dim, but the slow-speed operations of the period meant these lights were sufficient to allow crews to see the tracks and line-side obstructions at night.

Higher operating speeds and more-frequent night operations required more powerful lights by the turn of the 20th century. The solution was the electric light, which required another locomotive accessory, the on-board generator (also called "turbo-generator" or "dynamo"). These were provided by third-party suppliers—Pyle-National Co. (starting in 1897) and Sunbeam were two common manufacturers.

The dynamo was generally located atop the boiler in front of the cab, although locations varied among locomotives and railroads. They were powered by steam, with a valve in the cab that turned them on and off. In operation, their turbines emitted a distinctive high-pitched whine. They supplied a constant voltage (32 volts was common) for headlights, cab lights, and other uses.

Headlights were also provided by third-party manufacturers (Pyle, Sunbeam, Mars, and others). They came in many sizes, shapes, and styles, and many included built-in number boards along the sides or top. By the late steam era, twin sealed-beam headlights became common. Headlight style and placement varied widely among railroads, but individual railroads were often consistent about headlights across their own

Electric lights became common by 1900, and on modern locomotives like this Burlington Route 4-8-4 they could include signal lights or Mars lights similar to those on early diesels. Also note the automatic bell, classification lights at each corner, illuminated number boards mounted diagonally to the headlight, and the front number plate. *Art Stensvad; Jim Shaughnessy collection*

Former Gulf, Mobile & Northern 4-6-2 no. 425, with its bell ringing and classification lamps lit white to designate an extra train, approaches Schuylkill Haven on the former Reading line in December 2014. The locomotive is owned and operated by Blue Mountain & Reading/Reading & Northen in excursion service. *Brian Solomon*

The oil cup is a simple and effective means of providing continuous lubrication to reciprocating parts, using the force of gravity to move the oil. This view shows an older-style arrangement of brass oil cups with feed lines to supply oil to a locomotive's valve stem and piston rod. *Oren B. Helbok*

locomotives.

Number indicators or number boards, if not built as part of the headlight, were usually included at the top or front of the smokebox. These typically included three boards: one facing forward and one on each side at a 45-degree angle. As with other features, the board and number styles varied among railroads but were generally consistent on each railroad.

Classification lamps were used to indicate the status of a train: white for an extra; green for the first section of a train operating in multiple sections. In daytime, flags were used at each front corner of the locomotive (in built-in flag holders); at night, class lamps were illuminated; again, with a lamp at each front corner.

Lubrication and inspection

Steam locomotives, with their multitudes of moving parts and heavy exposed metal equipment, require continual lubrication to minimize friction, prevent oxidation, and ensure that components are free from unnecessary or unusual wear or stress.

Lubrication is required for all moving parts that rotate, rock, or slide back and forth.

Before locomotives began their daily journey and during scheduled stops, maintenance staff and/or locomotive crew members would carefully inspect running gear and other moving parts, while applying oil or grease to key points on the equipment. They would pay special attention to bearings and related components. Brasses must be checked to see if they are tightly in place, and nuts and bolts and pins on main rods, side rods, and related parts must be kept tight.

The traditional oil can was among the locomotive crew's standard equipment. Crews were cautioned to specifically direct lubricants to the correct places and not simply apply large quantities of oil all around the areas needing lubrication. In *Catechism of the Locomotive*, Forney instructed, "A few drops carefully introduced on a journal will do much more good than a large quantity poured on the part carelessly." Excessive oil on cylinders and valves can produce undesirable residue in the smokebox

Reading Class T-1 4-8-4 no. 2100 has a King model 31-8 Mechanical Lubricator. This was the smaller of two King model 31 types that used straight displacement pumps to supply oil to the locomotive's moving parts. The 31-8 could have up to 8 separate feed lines and had a 24-pint capacity. The oil reservoir is to the right of the lubricator, while the large cylindrical tank at far right is the main air reservoir. *Chris Bost*

It's necessary to keep all reciprocating parts well lubricated to avoid excessive wear and overheating. A Chicago & North Western employee lubricates drive rods using a Prime-Alemite Model 1063 Locomotive Rod Lubricator, manufactured by the Prime Manufacturing Co. *Trains magazine collection*

and exhaust stack. Excessive oiling on exposed areas will result in dirt and grime accumulation.

One of the oldest and most basic automatic lubrication systems was the oil cup. These were strategically placed near bearings, crossheads, cylinders, and on valve-box covers and other places where a gradual-but-constant flow of oil was necessary to ensure that parts remained lubricated while the locomotive was in motion. Oil cups were topped as required during station stops and inspections. Crosshead guides and connecting rods required close attention, and the oil in cups must be kept clean and free from debris so that oil was always free-flowing. When oiling bearings and crossheads, Forney advised, "There are no parts of a locomotive which require more careful attention in order to keep them lubricated, than thus prevent them from heating and being 'cut,' than the bearings on the crank pins and the slides of the crosshead. Examination should be made to see that neither the piston rods, pump-plungers, guides, connecting rods, nor crank pins are bent or sprung."

Likewise the valve gear required detailed attention. In Forney's time (mid-1870s) almost all locomotives still used inside valve gear, typically Stephenson, which made access difficult for key components that were located inside the engine frame. "All the bolts, nuts and keys should be carefully examined to see if they are properly fastened. The bolts and nuts in the eccentric straps are especially liable to become loose, and as they are between the wheels, and therefore not ease of access, are often neglected. The oil-holes should all be seen to be clear, otherwise it will be impossible to keep the journals well oiled. The eccentric

straps and the link blocks are very liable to be imperfectly oiled, and if the former become dry and cut, they throw great strain on the eccentric rods, which is liable to break them. When this occurs the strap and the portion of the rod which is attached to it revolve with the eccentric, and frequently a hole is thus knocked into the front of the firebox which disables the engine."

Alfred Bruce in his book *The Steam Locomotive in America* (published in 1950) offers a similar line of caution. "Obviously the proper lubrication of a larger modern steam locomotive and its auxiliaries still presents problems in spite of the very considerable advancement that has been made since 1900.

"A properly lubricated driving-axle journal presents a beautiful blue oily surface. This same surface when dry and unlubricated may become so hot that the surface skin of the journal will rupture in either circumferential or longitudinal characteristic 'heat checks' or both." The bottom line was that damage produced by the cutting edge of these heat checks could be catastrophic if left unattended.

Advanced lubrication equipment

Advanced automated lubrication equipment was invented to meet the specialized demands necessary for locomotive operation and running maintenance. Hydrostatic systems were developed in the 1850s and 1860s, but didn't become common in American practice until after 1880. After 1900, the invention of mechanical lubrication systems allowed for the quantity of lubrication to be matched proportionally to the speed of the engine.

Hydrostatic lubricators employed a small steam jet into a tightly contained oil

Booster engines are compact auxiliary steam engines that increased starting and slow-speed tractive effort. Common booster engine placement included locomotive trailing trucks and—as here—tender trucks. The 12-wheel tender on Missouri Pacific no. 1727 featured a rear-truck booster with external side rods to power both axles. *Louis A. Marre collection*

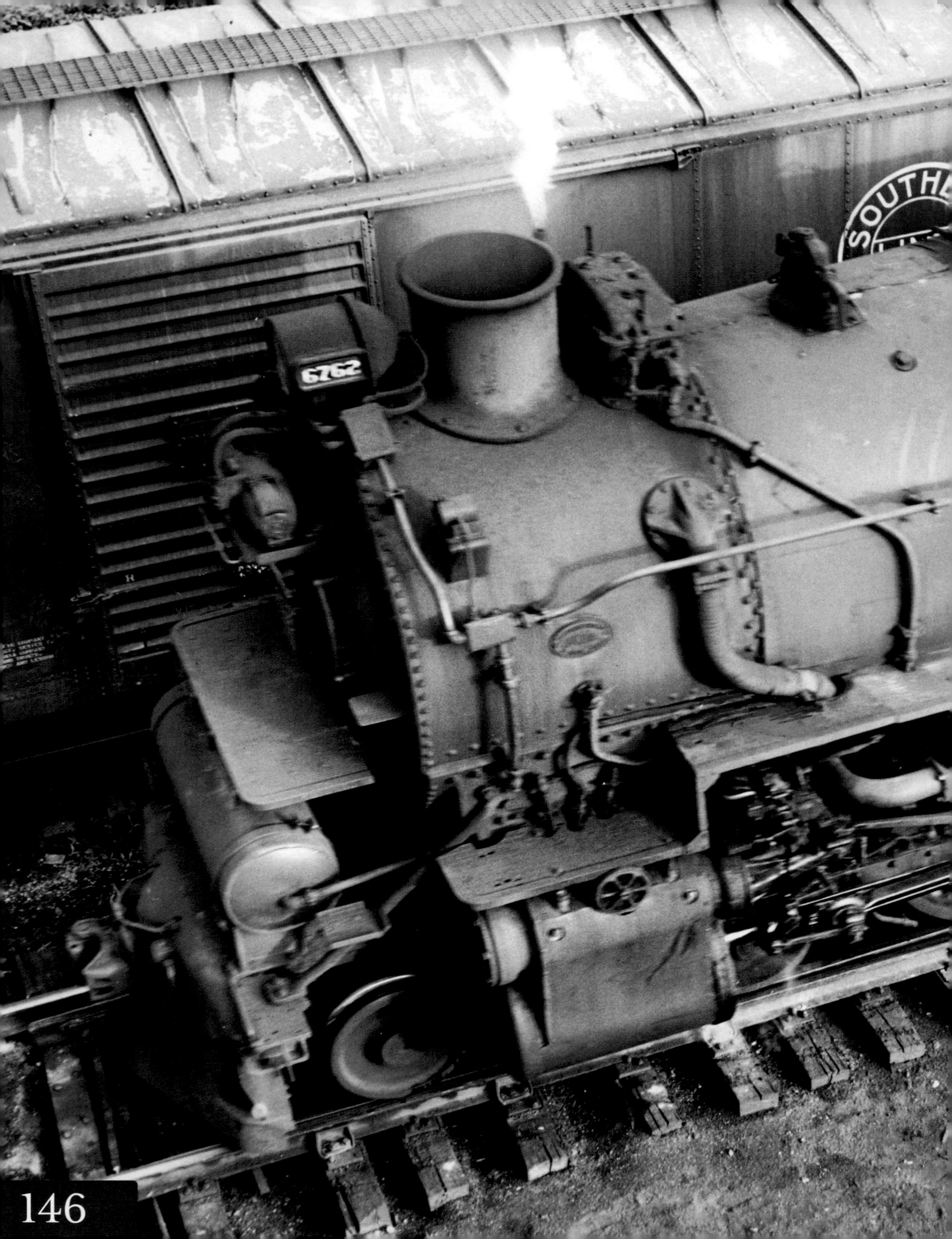
6762

Along the top of this Pennsylvania Railroad Mlb 4-8-2, from left to right: dynamo on platform in front of smokebox; headlight; exhaust stack; feedwater heater; automatic bell; sandbox (with two fill covers); steam dome (with throttle link) with whistle at rear; front of Belpaire firebox. *Don Wood*

Opposite bottom: **Milwaukee Road crew members pose with their 4-4-0 in the 1890s. Early locomotives had long, angled pilots. The metal bar lying on the prow is an extension for the link-and-pin coupler, allowing cars to be coupled to the locomotive in front of the pilot.** *Milwaukee Road*

Steam-actuated sanders are working on an Illinois Central locomotive. Sanding the rail increased adhesion and reduced wheel slip (when excessive power for rail conditions caused drive wheels to lose traction). *TRAINS magazine collection*

vessel. The natural effect of condensing steam in the vessel displaces oil, and the pressure distributes it via carefully placed feed lines to necessary points on the engine. The flow of oil may be varied by increasing or decreasing the volume of the steam jet. Control of the equipment is typically located on the back of the firebox in the locomotive cab, making it possible for crews to keep the engine properly lubricated while in motion. Mechanical lubrication systems often used a valve gear or crosshead connection to help determine the volume of lubricant necessary.

Both forms of automatic lubrication became more common as locomotives grew in size and power, and as traffic demands required longer and faster sustained operation that not only put greater stress on equipment but provided fewer opportunities for manual lubrication and inspection.

Third-party manufacturers engaged in the design and production of automated locomotive lubricators. A common type was the Nathan D.V. Mechanical Lubricator, made by the Nathan Manufacturing Company of New York, which had been in the business of supplying lubrication equipment since the 1860s. The Type D.V. was a valveless machine driven by a crosshead connection. It was designed to automatically oil inlet and outlet openings, using a plunger to create suction to deliver oil. This device featured a heating chamber to maintain oil in a fluid state in cold weather. It used strainers in the oil reservoirs to filter foreign matter from oil before delivery to locomotive surfaces.

The Detroit Lubricator Company advertised its Bullseye Locomotive Lubricator as an advanced type of machine manufactured in various sizes with up to eight separate feed lines. The primary component was a one-piece casting designed

to minimize the number of components and thus limit the instances of the system breaking down. It used a complex network of cast internal passages. Description of its operation explains the value of this machine as it was sold in the early 1920s, but also reveals the failings its technological antecedents:

"An oil control valve in the oil passage between the reservoir and sign feed regulating valves—a distinctive feature of the Detroit Bullseye Locomotive Lubricator—places in the hands of the operator a means of instantly starting, stopping or throttling the rate of feed, so does away with the necessity of shutting off the feed regulating valves at a terminal or when refilling on the road and consequently the necessity of opening and readjusting these valves after refilling or at the commencement of a service movement. It provides for the closing of cylinder feeds,

Common whistle signals

Sound	Indication
o	Apply brakes. Stop.
— —	Release brakes. Proceed.
o o o	When standing, back.
— — o	Approaching meeting or waiting points.
— o o o	Flagman protect rear of train.
o o o —	Flagman protect front of train.
— — — —	Flagman may return from west or south.
— — — — —	Flagman may return from east or north.
— — —	Train parted; to be repeated until answered
o o	Answer to any signal not otherwise provided for.
o o o o	Call for signal.
— — o —	Approaching public crossings at grade.

o = short sound
— = long sound

Solid cast pilots became common in the 1930s. They were often used with retractable couplers (especially on passenger locomotives), as here on a Milwaukee Road 4-6-2 in 1936. *Milwaukee Road*

be engaged at speeds up to about 20 mph, and remain engaged up to about 30 mph. The booster was especially useful in getting heavy trains moving and preventing heavy trains from stalling while ascending a steep gradient. However, its geared connections generally contributed to relatively high maintenance costs which limited their application.

Boosters were applied on a variety of large late-era locomotives with mixed results; they were a common feature of many early Super-Power locomotives. Adding a booster allowed for a locomotive's higher starting tractive effort in published figures. Because of this, when a booster was used, it was qualified in a locomotive's official specifications. Tractive-effort figures were often listed with and without booster engines to avoid any confusion as to the output of a specific locomotive.

Franklin Railway Supply Company of New York was a primary supplier of trailing truck boosters. It described its locomotive booster as a "two-cylinder 90-degree engine, the dimension being controlled by the weight on the axle which it drives. Attached to the frame of the truck though a three-point suspension, the Booster transmits its power to the driven axle through an idler gear which can be engaged or disengaged at the will of the operator, within the speed range of [the] Booster. Its speed is controlled by [a] mechanism attached to the reverse gear quadrant so when the cutoff of the main engine is shortened after a pre-determined speed has been reached the Booster cuts out automatically."

Sand

The application of clean, dry stand on the rail in front of driving wheels was an early established means of improving wheel-rail adhesion. This was necessary to prevent wheel slip in adverse conditions such as when water, oil, or debris (such as grass, weeds, or dead leaves) covered the rail, and was especially useful when starting or on steep grades. Slipping drivers make starting a locomotive difficult, and can contribute to a train stalling on a grade.

The most common type of sand storage was in a dome-shaped box atop and astride the boiler. The sand box (sometimes called a sand dome) was usually forward of the steam dome; the sand box can be identified by the sand-fill access hatches atop it. Pipes routed sand downward, ending just forward and aft of the main driver (and sometimes additional drivers). Some locomotives had two sand boxes, each serving one or two driver sets.

Early sanders relied on gravity; later locomotives used pneumatic controls, with air supplied from the main air reservoir and controlled with a three-way valve in the cab. In addition to delivering sand through delivery pipes, pneumatic systems often allowed for a blast of air through the pipes to purge obstructions. Sand boxes were replenished during routine servicing;

Poling pockets allowed crews to use poles to shove cars on adjoining tracks. The practice was dangerous (and was eventually banned), but it could be a time-saver for crews. *Trains magazine collection*

Switching locomotives were required to have footboards on the front pilot. Here two crewmen ride the footboards of a Union Pacific 0-4-0 at Los Angeles in 1957.
Robert A. Trennert

4439

The steel running board on Canadian Pacific 4-6-2 2317 has a handrail above it, but the pipe along the platform could be a hazard for walking along it. *Brian Solomon*

Opposite: **This view shows the steps leading from the pilot to the running board, along with a raised platform on the pilot for accessing the headlight.** *Milwaukee Road*

sanding towers were usually located at locomotive fueling and maintenance facilities.

Pilots

The main job of a locomotive pilot is to clear any obstructions from the track, hopefully knocking them to the side before they could wind up under the wheels and cause damage or a derailment. Pilots were made in many styles and sizes. On many early locomotives they were long and angled; their prominence gave them the nickname "cowcatcher."

In the days of link-and-pin couplers these worked well, and most had a long bar attached to the pilot beam (behind the pilot) with a loop at the end that could be extended when coupling to cars at the front. As air brakes were installed, long air hoses were typically added to the pilot as well. The knuckle coupler first appeared in the 1870s (Eli Janney received his patent in 1873) but it wasn't until the Railroad Safety Appliance Act of 1893 that knuckle couplers became mandatory (as well as air brakes, both with a 1900 target date).

The long pilots proved impractical with the transition to knuckle couplers by the 1890s, as the coupler shank could not be extended that far. Although typical pilots shrunk in size, most retained the same angular design, a shallow V-shaped prow with individual spokes extending outward from the pilot beam. These spokes were often made from old boiler tubes recycled for the purpose (and were sometimes called "boiler-tube pilots." Many modern locomotives had cast-steel (non-spoked) pilots of various designs.

The front coupler was mounted on the pilot beam, with a shank long enough to clear the pilot. Uncoupling levers were of many designs, but most have a steel rod extending across the pilot beam, with

OCT. 26 - 1931

A ladder was required on the rear (or side rear corner) of the tender. This view of a Delaware & Hudson tender also shows the grab irons, cast corner steps, backup light, marker lights, passenger steam line connection (left of the coupler), and air brake and signal hoses (right of the coupler; the smaller signal hose is tucked behind the brake hose). Stenciling indicates water and coal capacity. *Trains magazine collection*

curved handles on either end. Lifting the lever releases the uncoupling pin and opens the knuckle.

Some locomotives had retractable front couplers, usually built to be part of a cast pilot. Streamlined appearance was their goal, and they were most common on streamlined passenger engines but could be found on freight locomotives as well (the Big Boy, for example). Along with appearance, they were safer—a large obstruction (such as an automobile) hit at high speed could get hung up on the coupler and cause a derailment. However, in practice, retractable couplers sometimes proved to be more trouble than they were worth; some railroads eventually eliminated them or simply left them in the open position.

On switching locomotives, pilots with footboards were required in place of the traditional angled front. This provided a place for brakemen to ride while performing switching moves (a dangerous practice that was eventually banned in the diesel era, but widely done in steam days). The footboard had to be at least 10" deep, with a vertical backstop, and could be in two parts (with a gap under the coupler) or could extend all the way across the pilot. Switchers also were required to have footboards on the rear of the tender as well.

The brake system air hose was also mounted on the pilot next to the coupler, and passenger locomotives would likely have a steam line connection (on the side opposite the air hose) and a signal line air hose (next to the brake hose).

Poling pockets were also found on the outside corners of the pilot beams (they were found on freight cars of the era as well). These were small, rimmed, circular indentations used sometimes in a switching procedure called "poling." This enabled a locomotive to move a car on an adjoining track by placing a pole between poling pockets on the locomotive and car as the photo on page 153 shows. It's a dangerous practice and was eventually banned, but crews in the steam era did it on occasion to save time while switching.

Ladders, running boards, handholds

Locomotives have a variety of ladders, steps, and grab irons. Their use and placement varied into the 1900s but became required and standardized by an amendment of the Safety Act in 1911 (and specifics were modified in 1915 and later amendments). Steps were located at each tender corner and at the ends of the locomotive pilot beam. Grab irons ("handholds") are required at many locations, namely above all steps and footboards and above the running board. Ladders were required on the rear of all tenders.

Running boards are located on each side of the boiler to allow access to appliances mounted atop and along the boiler. These were to be a minimum of 10" wide; they could be stepped (sections at different levels) depending upon the shape and size of the boiler and the location of other appliances. Early versions were often wood; later running boards were metal with tread plates, with open grating on many modern locomotives. If the front of the running board was at a high level, access steps would be added down to the pilot. A handrail was required above the running board, to be placed 24" to 66" above the board.

308
20,000 GALS
25 TONS

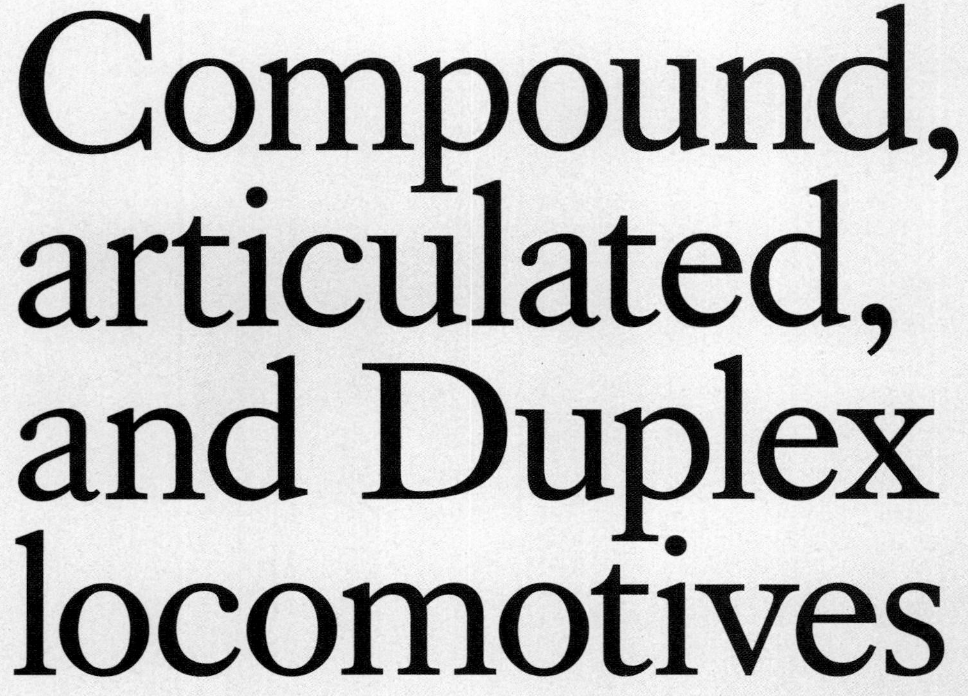

Chapter 7

Compound, articulated, and Duplex locomotives

The 0-6-6-0 Mallet compound was designed for slow-speed service moving very heavy freight. Kansas City Southern no. 700 works a long freight in Louisiana in August 1934. The large low-pressure cylinders on the forward engine are typical of the Mallet arrangement. Number 700 was one of a dozen 0-6-6-0s built by Alco for the railroad in 1912. *Harold Vollrath; Brian Solomon collection*

As locomotives became larger and more powerful, designers looked for ways to increase power while making more-efficient use of steam. One early popular method was compounding—using steam twice to capture more of its energy before expelling it to the atmosphere. The most-successful compounds were large articulated Mallets. As steam technology advanced, these were followed by large simple (non-compound) articulated locomotives.

Compound engines

As chapter 3 explained, in a conventional steam engine, pressurized steam is injected into a cylinder, where it expands to act on a piston during the power stroke; on the return piston stroke, this steam is exhausted into the atmosphere. Although locomotives are double acting, meaning steam acts upon the piston in both directions, the overall use of steam is inefficient because it is exhausted while it still has considerable expansive power remaining.

A more-efficient use of steam is a multiple-expansion engine, typically known as a "compound." Compound engines increase efficiency by using multiple-stage expansion to extract more energy from the steam—essentially using it twice—before exhausting it into the atmosphere. To do

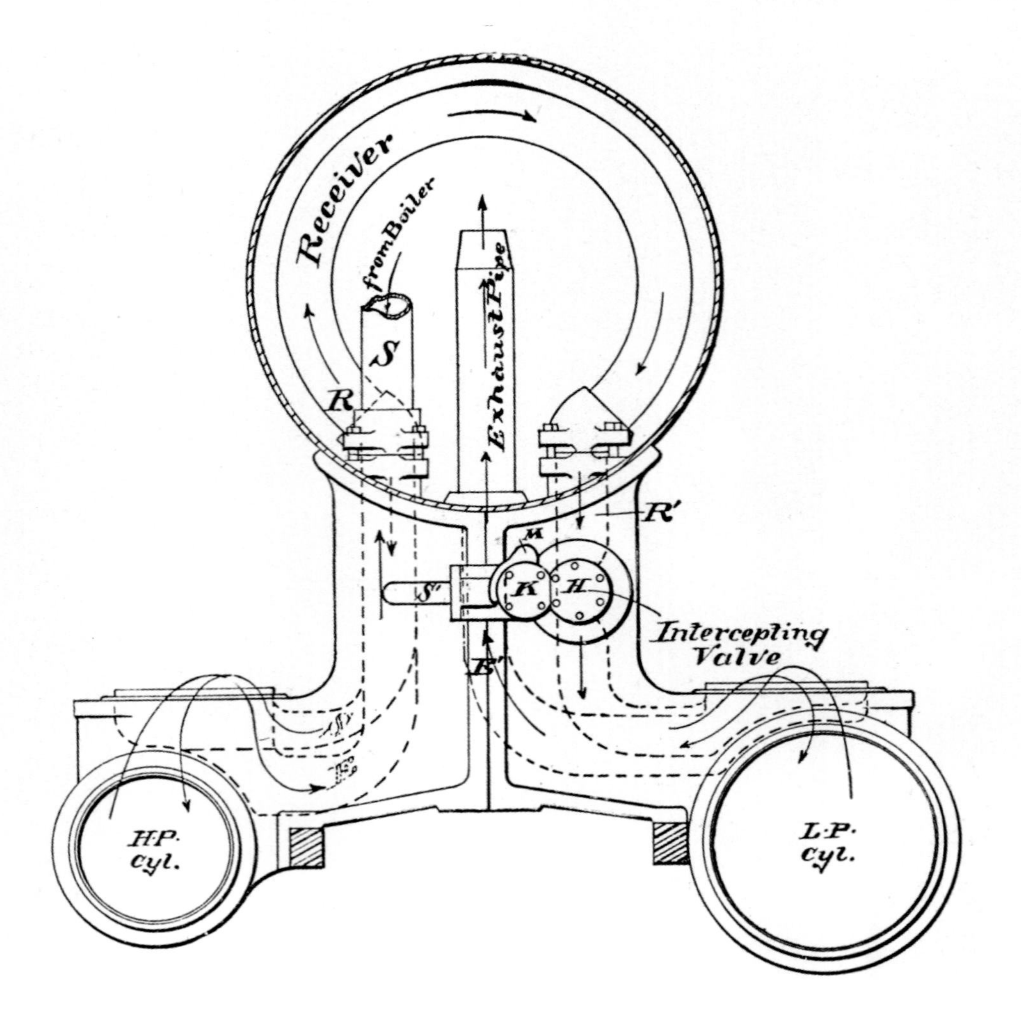

This 1890s cross-section diagram, from Kirkman's *The Compound Locomotive*, shows the cylinder arrangement, location of interceptor valve, and steam flow for a Schenectady two-cylinder compound locomotive. It nicely illustrates the concept of compounding: steam that's exhausted from the small high-pressure cylinder (left) is kept in the system and recirculated to supply the large low-pressure cylinder (right).

this on a locomotive, the exhaust steam from the first (high-pressure) cylinder is routed to a low-pressure cylinder, where it drives another piston. A key trade-off is that—because the steam has used some of its expansive power—to provide the equivalent power output in the second cylinder, the diameter of the low-pressure cylinder must be significantly larger than the first (high-pressure) cylinder.

British and other European railroads were early to take advantage of operating compound designs, albeit with mixed results. Among the first American compounds was an experimental tandem compound locomotive built in the 1860s from the parts of an earlier engine by the Shepard Iron Works in Buffalo, N.Y. By the 1880s, when American railroads were facing rapid traffic growth and railroads sought improved efficiency and greater power, it seemed that compounding offered an improved solution in being able to move greater tonnage with a single locomotive.

Locomotive builders and railroads began trying various wheel and mechanical arrangements to make the best use of the compounding principle. Initially, several non-articulated compound designs were used; these were built commercially from the late-1880s until about 1910 (although the popularity of the type peaked about 1900). Beginning in 1904, adaptations of the European articulated (Mallet) compound locomotives found favor in the U.S., and these soon became the most common type of compound locomotive in American practice.

The main advantage of compounding was increased efficiency: a locomotive could be more powerful while using the same amount of steam as a simple (non-compound) locomotive with the same boiler/grate/firebox combination. Better draft, and thus

New York Central & Hudson River 2-8-0 no. 2500 was built by Schenectady in 1901 and assigned to the Boston & Albany for freight service. This two-cylinder cross-compound featured a large-diameter low-pressure cylinder on the engineer's side and a small-diameter high-pressure cylinder on the fireman's side. Unequal power to the respective cylinders when starting led enginemen to refer to this type of locomotive in less-than-complimentary terms as a "slam-bang." *Robert A. Buck collection, courtesy of Ken Buck*

Santa Fe no. 988 is a 2-10-0 built as a compound by Alco in 1901. It originally had a 17.5 x 30 cylinder on the right side and a 30 x 34 cylinder on the left. As with most cross-compound locomotives, it was eventually simpled (in 1915); it's shown here after conversion. *H.P. Middlebrook*

more efficient fire, is another advantage, as noted by Marshall Kirkman in his 1899 book *The Compound Locomotive.*

However, there were several downsides as well. Compound locomotives were significantly more mechanically complex, which increased maintenance costs and service times. It was difficult to precisely match the power outputs between the high- and low-pressure cylinders, which could lessen efficiency. Operation was also more challenging: On starting, most compounds allowed crews to inject high-pressure steam into both low- and high-pressure cylinders. Crews had to switch back to compound operation at the proper time, or efficiency would drop and—in extreme cases—damage could result.

Compounding eventually fell out of favor, with builders and railroads moving toward larger simple locomotives with higher boiler pressures, superheaters, and larger grate areas and fireboxes that could produce more steam more efficiently. These had fewer mechanical challenges compared to compound locomotives.

Innovative locomotive designers devised myriad designs for compound arrangements, employing combinations of two, three, and four cylinders. Compound designers aimed to minimize mechanical complexity while providing for equivalent output between high- and low-pressure cylinders and compensating for the unequal stresses on equipment that resulted from the differences in cylinder output. Each arrangement offered different solutions to these problems. Let's take a look at some of the designs.

Baldwin Vauclain Compound

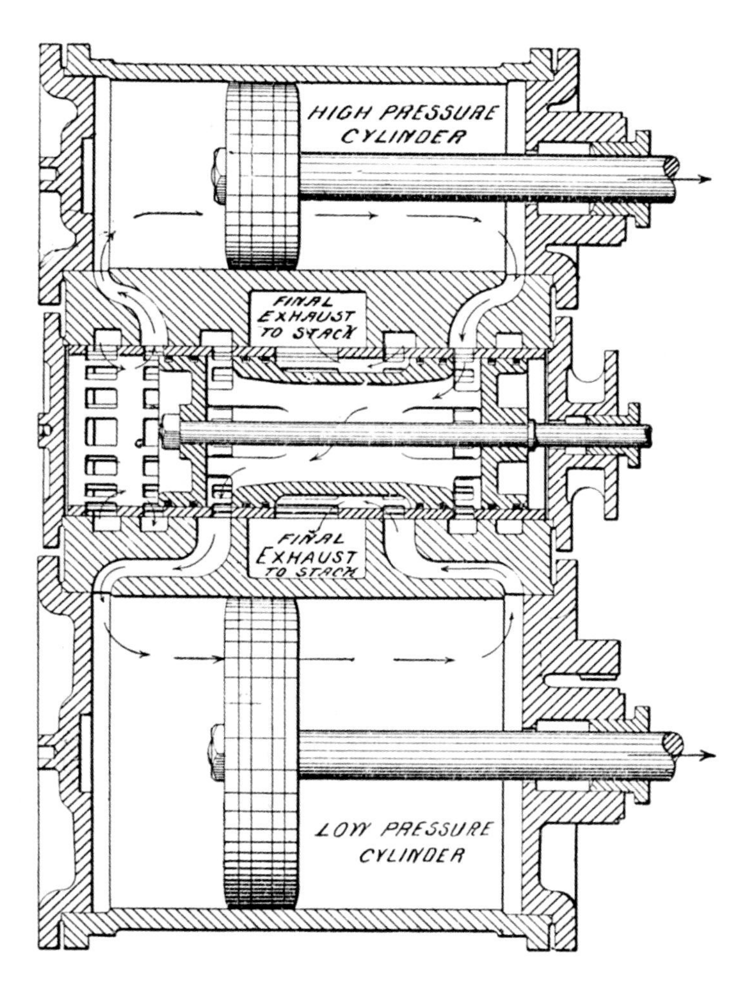

The idea of the Vauclain compound is a high- and low-pressure cylinder paired on the same side of the locomotive, with a piston valve between them. *Baldwin*

Two-cylinder cross-compound

The cross-compound locomotive is a two-cylinder arrangement featuring a single high-pressure cylinder on one side of the engine opposite a low-pressure cylinder on the other. Because the low-pressure cylinder needed to equal the power of the high-pressure cylinder, the low-pressure cylinder used a substantially larger diameter which resulted in an unbalanced, asymmetrical appearance that was distinctive.

Schenectady Locomotive Works was among the leading builder of two-cylinder cross-compound locomotives. The company promoted its design as an automatic compound benefiting from an intercepting valve and a receiver. Kirkman described the operation: "In starting the engine, a small pipe from the boiler through a reducing valve supplied steam to the low-pressure cylinder at a reduced pressure. When the receiver had accumulated sufficient pressure by the exhaust into it from the high-pressure cylinder, the intercepting valve would automatically be thrown to its normal position for working compound; then the supply of live steam to the low-pressure cylinder was cut off and the receiver pressure admitted, and thus the engine worked [as a] compound."

An improved design of intercepting valve introduced in 1892 improved the performance of Schenectady compound locomotives, but in actual practice,

This view of Milwaukee Road Vauclain compound 4-4-2 no. 915 shows the ends of the cylinders and the valve chambers (set to the inside). It was built in 1901 and scrapped in 1927. *Milwaukee Road*

Union Pacific 2-8-0 no. 1635 is a Baldwin Vauclain compound built in 1900. It has the low-pressure cylinder atop the high-pressure cylinder. It would be rebuilt to a simple engine in 1910. *Trains magazine collection*

operation of Schenectady cross-compounds didn't prove as smooth as its designers had hoped. On the Boston & Albany, cross-compound engines were known to engine crews as "slam-bangs," a term that vividly described their motion. These compounds had short service lives.

Three-cylinder locomotives

Various arrangements of three-cylinder compound engines gained favor in Britain and Europe, typically involving a center cylinder powering a cranked axle. Except for a few experimental locomotives, notably those built by the Reading Company, the three-cylinder compound type was largely ignored in North America.

In the 1920s, Alco promoted three-cylinder simple locomotives with high-pressure steam directed to all cylinders. These were tried by several railroads, with Union Pacific's fleet of enormous 9000-series 4-12-2s being the largest (and most successful) of the type (see pages 92 and 93 in Chapter 3).

Non-articulated four-cylinder compound

Non-articulated four-cylinder compound locomotives offered a variety of advantages over two-cylinder compounds. Depending on the arrangement, these could either deliver greater crosshead thrust or divide piston thrusts over a greater number of impulses.

The four-cylinder tandem compound was developed by the Brooks Works in the early 1890s and was promoted as providing a more even piston thrust than cross-compound designs. A tandem compound is defined by pair of cylinders on each side of the locomotive with the high-pressure cylinder placed immediately in front of a low-pressure cylinder, with the two connected via a common piston rod. On each side of the engine, a single piston valve regulated steam admission for high- and low-pressure cylinders. These tended to have better maintenance records than cross-compounds, as the straight-forward cylinder configuration and common crosshead

This Great Northern 4-4-2 Atlantic is a rare example of a Baldwin four-cylinder balanced compound with a Belpaire boiler. Built in 1906, it was one of 10 such engines ordered by GN. High-pressure cylinders inside the frame powered the first set of drivers via a crank axle, while the outside-frame low-pressure cylinders powered the second set of drivers using main rods. *Brian Solomon collection*

obviated much of the complexity associated with other compound types. Santa Fe in particular bought a large number of tandems for heavy freight work.

However, this cylinder arrangement experienced problems with packing material between high- and low-pressure cylinders. Cylinder maintenance was also more involved because of the greater difficulties in accessing the low-pressure cylinder (doing so required removal of the high-pressure components). Another design problem was difficulty in counterbalancing a tandem's greater reciprocating weight—one reason why the type was primarily for slow-speed freight locomotives.

The most successful non-articulated four-cylinder arrangement was Baldwin's Vauclain compound, named for its inventor, Samuel Vauclain, who patented his design in 1889. This type is distinguished by locating the high- and low-pressure cylinders one on top of the other on the same side of the locomotive with a common cross-head connection, with a cylindrical piston valve to provide steam admission to both cylinders. This gave the Vauclain compound its distinctive appearance, with a triple cylindrical cluster on each side of the engine.

Vauclain compounds were among the earliest commercially produced locomotives to make widespread use of the piston valve (explained in Chapter 3). Piston valves

were favored because they allowed for superior valve and port arrangements that were necessitated by an unusually complex steam passage arrangement that was an important part of the Vauclain design. This permitted a relatively simple valve motion and minimized the necessity for complicated mechanical equipment. The cylinders and valve chambers were cast as a single unit, while valves featured a double-ended hollow design.

A primary advantage of the Vauclain design was that each side of the engine had equal power, which gave this locomotive most of the favorable characteristics associated with a simple engine, but with drafting and power advantages of a compound. It featured superior reciprocating equipment that was better balanced and thus suitable to operate at higher speeds (including passenger service as well as heavy freight work). Although Vauclain compounds were capable of working fast, they were most efficient at more conservative speeds.

The specific cylinder/valve arrangement was dependent on the size of the cylinders and driving wheels and the clearance requirements for each railroad. Locomotives with large-diameter driving wheels were arranged with low-pressure cylinders below the high-pressure cylinders; by contrast, freight locomotives with small-diameter drivers had high-pressure cylinders below in

order to accommodate tight clearances.

In order to limit problems caused by low-pressure-cylinder back pressure (which tended to develop at higher speeds), Vauclain compounds tended to have their valves set for a short maximum cutoff that limited steam admission to the cylinders. Since a large-diameter driver required fewer piston strokes to reach a desired top speed, passenger Vauclains featured considerably larger driving wheels than typical comparable simple locomotives. Vauclain compounds used a starting valve to work the engine, with high-pressure steam to all cylinders to start, and at other times where greater power might be necessary (such as climbing heavy grades at slow speeds).

Unlike the cross-compounds described earlier, the Vauclain's starting valve did not employ an interceptor. So when it was working as a simple engine, low-pressure cylinders performed a greater share of the work owing to their larger piston size. However, this starting arrangement

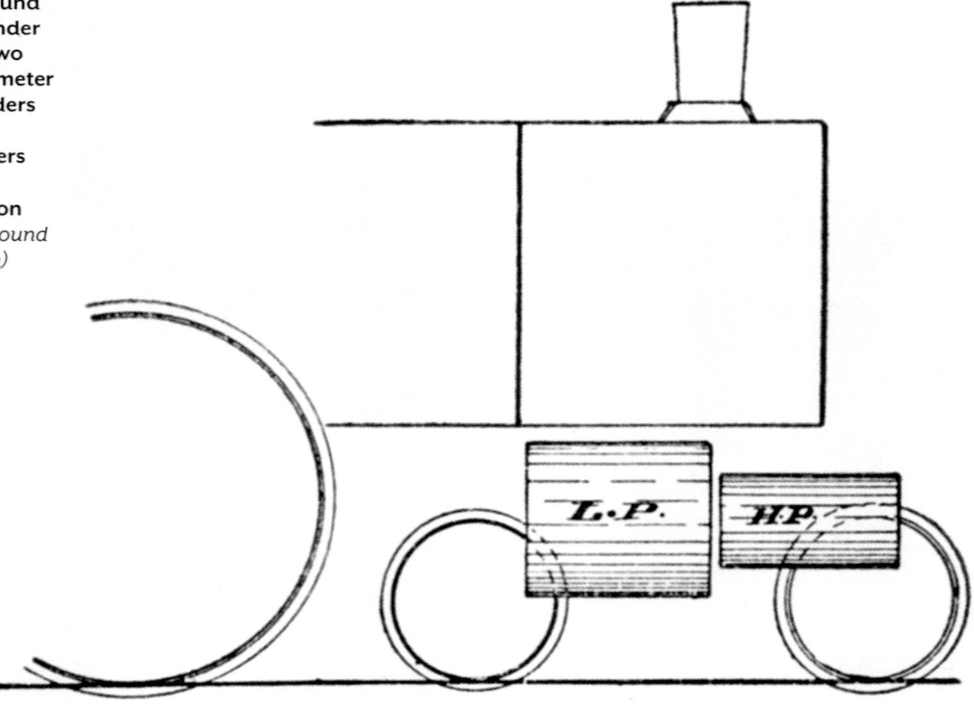

The tandem compound featured a four-cylinder arrangement with two groups of small-diameter high-pressure cylinders and high-diameter low pressure cylinders arranged in tandem coupled to a common drive rod. *The Compound Locomotive (Kirkman)*

was viewed as a disadvantage since the low-pressure cylinders took on a greater proportion of the thrust and placed a disproportionate strain on crossheads, tending to push them out of alignment. This could result in excessive wear to both crossheads and guides while causing leaks to piston rod packing.

Although many Vauclain compounds were built until just after 1900, railroads eventually found that maintenance issues and expenses negated the improved efficiency and performance. Most were rebuilt as simple locomotives in the 1910s and 1920s, with others scrapped.

A more-advanced four-cylinder design was the balanced compound. This gained favor with European railways in the late 19th century, and was imported and adapted to American practice in the early 20th century.

French locomotive designer Alfred G. DeGlehn invented a popular type of four-cylinder, four-crank balanced compound that featured all four cylinders positioned in a horizontal row, and with four crank points instead of two. In the most common arrangement, two high-pressure cylinders were located inside the locomotive frame powering lead driving wheels via a cranked axle; the low-pressure cylinders were located outside the frame in a more conventional position with external rods connected via outside crank pins to a second set of drivers.

The success of this type led Samuel Vauclain to refine a similar arrangement known as the Baldwin Balanced Compound. It was better balanced than most earlier American compound types, which was a function of the piston and cranked-axle arrangement. This facilitated parallel high- and low-pressure pistons traveling in

In the 1920s and 1930s, more than a decade after commercial builders had largely abandoned development of non-articulated compound types, Delaware & Hudson designed a series of unusual but advanced high-pressure compounds that featured water tube boilers and extremely high steam pressure to achieve superior thermal efficiency. Number 1402 used a cross-compound cylinder arrangement. Its high pressure required special lubrication and delivery equipment. *J.R. Quinn collection*

4043
4043
SOUTHERN PACIFIC
S
4043

ERIE
MATT H SHAY

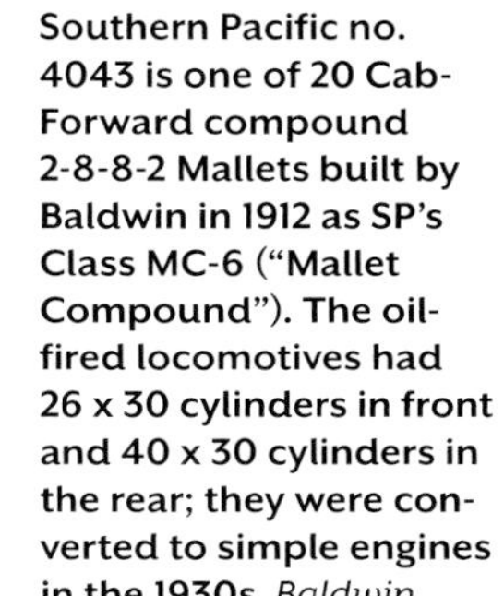
Southern Pacific no. 4043 is one of 20 Cab-Forward compound 2-8-8-2 Mallets built by Baldwin in 1912 as SP's Class MC-6 ("Mallet Compound"). The oil-fired locomotives had 26 x 30 cylinders in front and 40 x 30 cylinders in the rear; they were converted to simple engines in the 1930s. *Baldwin*

Erie experimented with a Triplex 2-8-8-8-2, with three built by Baldwin in 1914, as slow-speed helper locomotives. The third (rear) engine was located under the tender. They suffered from many problems, mainly a difficulty in generating steam quickly enough, and only lasted a few years in service. *Erie*

opposite directions to one another, which improved weight distribution while reducing the damaging effects from reciprocating forces. Another benefit was the greater number of impulses per driving wheel revolution, which lowered stresses on drive rods and related parts.

On the downside, the locomotive's more complicated equipment tended to increase maintenance and repair costs. This was especially acute with the cranked axle and interior cylinders. As with earlier compounds, costs negated the advantages offered by smoother operation and fuel savings. As result, relatively few balanced compounds were built in the U.S.

Mallet articulated

The articulated Mallet compound was adapted for heavy American operations from a compact narrow gauge European design. The type dated to the 1880s, when Anatole Mallet (pronounced "malley") patented his original articulated compound locomotive. This arrangement effectively placed two sets of running gear (two engines) with a hinged frame under a single boiler. The rear engine (set of drivers) was rigid with the boiler frame; the front engine could pivot, or articulate, under the front of the boiler, allowing the locomotive to negotiate curves.

The first U.S. Mallet was built by Alco for Baltimore & Ohio in 1904. It featured an 0-6-6-0 wheel arrangement and briefly held the title of the "heaviest and most powerful locomotive." As with most subsequent American Mallets, the rear engine featured a pair of high-pressure cylinders which exhausted into low-pressure cylinders on the forward engine. Similar to Mallet's original design, B&O's Mallet required two sets of frames, one for each set of running gear, using a hinged arrangement with a pivot joint. The rear frames were rigidly aligned to

The 2-6-6-2 wheel arrangement was the most common applied to the Mallet compound, yet Burlington 4107, at Denver in July 1935, was a very unusual machine. It was one of 10 class T-2 compounds built for the railroad by Baldwin in 1910. Originally designed to burn low-yield lignite coal, the T-2s featured two-section boilers with the front portion serving as a feedwater heater. Number 4107 was among T-2s rebuilt as an oil-burner and equipped with an Elesco feedwater heater (behind the headlight atop of the smokebox). *Joseph Schick; Robert A. Buck collection*

The largest cylinders ever applied to a steam locomotive were the 48" low-pressure cylinders on the front engine of Virginian 2-10-10-2s, including no. 802. Ten were built by Alco in 1918; some survived in service into the late 1950s. *Trains magazine collection.*

Not all Mallets were large locomotives. Many smaller locomotives, like this Baldwin 2-6-6-2 built for Weyerhaeuser, were designed to operate on tight curves and steep grades. *Baldwin*

the boiler and the front frames supported the boiler with a sliding bearing surface, with flexible steam pipes delivering live steam to the front cylinders.

Articulation allowed the locomotive to work effectively on lines with sharp curves and enabled a much more powerful locomotive than would have been possible using a rigid wheelbase. The 0-6-6-0 lacked front pilot wheels, which limited the engine's operation when leading trains in road service. Most 0-6-6-0s were built as helper engines or for slow-speed service. Later Mallets benefited from the addition of leading wheels for road service.

Despite its unconventional appearance, B&O's pioneer proved to be an immediate success and led to the Mallet compound rapidly gaining favor with American lines just as interest in non-articulated compounds was waning. The estimated 2,400 Mallets built in the U.S. made the type by far the most common American compound locomotive of the 20th century. They were almost all slow-speed, heavy-service freight locomotives.

Significantly, B&O's first locomotive offered technological precedents for U.S. steam practice. It reintroduced the benefits of Walschaerts outside valve gear (see Chapter 3), which over the next decade supplanted traditional inside valve gear as the preferred type of valve gear for most new road locomotives. The Walschaerts design offered greater accessibility, lower motion stress, and reduced wear. The locomotive also pioneered power-reverse gear, equipment later adopted as standard by most builders as locomotives grew larger.

The Mallet nickname was applied to almost all articulated compound locomotives, regardless of wheel arrangement. The majority of American Mallets were 2-6-6-2s or 2-8-8-2s. The Mallet also achieved extreme proportions with unusual wheel arrangements adopted for specific applications on several railroads. Santa Fe and Virginian bought 2-10-10-2s; Santa Fe's were short-lived and were soon rebuilt into smaller locomotives, but Virginian's 2-10-10-2s had long service lives, lasting into the 1950s. Built by Alco in 1918, each weighed 684,000 pounds and had 30 x 32-inch low pressure cylinders with 48 x 32-inch low pressure cylinders—the largest ever used on a locomotive. Like most

In 1907 Erie bought powerful locomotives for helper service over Gulf Summit (east of Susquehanna, Pa.). These included the only Mallet Camelbacks: three massive Alco-built 0-8-8-0s with large, wide Wooten fireboxes and separate cabs for engineer and fireman. *Brian Solomon collection*

Unlike Mallets or simple articulated locomotive types, a Duplex features a divided drive on a fixed frame. Pennsylvania class Q2 6181, a 4-4-6-4, is at Crestline, Ohio on Oct. 5, 1947. It was among the most powerful non-articulated locomotives ever built, delivering almost 8,000 horsepower.
E. Lensberger, Jay Williams collection

Duplex locomotives

Olex-drive steam locomotives have two engines (two sets of drivers) under a common boiler, so at first glance they look like an articulated locomotive; however, they have rigid frames, so they are non-articulated. The Baltimore & Ohio built the first Duplex in the U.S. in the mid-1930s, a 4-4-4-4 (which it built after rejecting a Baldwin proposal). The goal was to create a better-balanced, more-powerful locomotive than was possible with a conventional long-wheelbase rigid-frame locomotive. By dividing drivers into groups, rods could be lighter, lessening problems with balancing reciprocating weight. The B&O's locomotive was not successful.

The Pennsylvania Railroad became the prime customer and developer of the Duplex type, starting with a single S1-class 6-6-4-6 developed with Baldwin in 1939. Next was the passenger-service T1-class 4-4-4-4, with two delivered by Baldwin in 1942 and 50 production locomotives in 1945. A lone Q1, a 4-6-4-4, was built in 1942 for fast freight service; Pennsy then followed by building 25 modified (4-4-6-4) Q2 locomotives in 1945.

The resulting locomotives were indeed powerful; the Pennsy's Q2s were the most-powerful rigid-frame locomotives on U.S. rails. However, the locomotives were prone to slipping (simplified, the two sets of drivers tended to fight with each other). Mechanically they were complex—having two sets of drivers and related cylinders, valve gear, and other equipment negated the gains of the additional power—and spent more time in the shops than anticipated. Their long frames were also problematic, limiting the areas where they could operate.

The Q2s were the most successful Duplex locomotive, but by the time they and the T1s were delivered, further developments, modifications, or refinements were a moot point: conventional articluateds (such as the Challenger, Allegheny, and Big Boy) had shown they could be both fast and powerful, without the mechanical challenges of the Duplex; and both types were doomed by dieselization, which by 1945 was inevitable and well on its way.

This Baltimore & Ohio class EL-2 2-8-8-0, built by Baldwin in 1917, was among several locomotives the B&O rebuilt in the late 1920s as simple articulateds (note that the front and rear cylinders are the same size). This was a common modification for many older Mallets. Many of these locomotives served into the 1950s. *Robert A. Buck collection*

Union Pacific's Challengers (4-6-6-4s) helped demonstrate that simple articulateds could be fast as well as powerful, and worked in both passenger and freight service. These big engines benefited from an articulated frame with a modern bearing surface between the forward engine and boiler that enabled them to work most UP main lines. *Robert A. Witbeck, collection of the Center for Railroad Photography & Art*

compounds, Virginian's 2-10-10-2s were capable of operating as single expansion engines when starting. When working simple they were rated at 176,600 pounds of tractive effort—the greatest tractive effort of any reciprocating steam locomotive ever built. As compounds, their tractive effort figure was 147,200 pounds. They were used to move coal trains weighing up to 17,050 tons without a helper—a phenomenal amount of tonnage hauled by one locomotive in the World War I era, and the figure remains impressive even to this day.

Southern Pacific ordered a unique variation of the Mallet that effectively reversed the orientation of the locomotive, known as the Cab-Forward. This was facilitated by an oil-burning design that allowed the firebox to be at the opposite end of the boiler from the tender, because the fuel could be piped from the tender.

The Cab-Forward was SP's solution to a difficult operating problem. SP had ordered early 2-8-8-2s, but soon found that when

Some Mallets were built late in the steam era. The Norfolk & Western built this class Z1b 2-6-6-2 Mallet compound in 1942, and it's working as a pusher at Blue Ridge Summit east of Roanoke, Va., in the summer of 1955. *Robert A. Witbeck, collection of the Center for Railroad Photography & Art*

Following Southern Pacific's initial Cab-Forward Mallets came orders for non-compound articulated locomotives. This is Baldwin-built class AC-4 4-8-8-2 no. 4100, pictured with its crew. It was built in 1928. *C. Edward Hedstrom; Brian Solomon collection*

The massive 4-8-8-4 Big Boy was unique to Union Pacific, with a total of only 25 built. This view from the early 1950s shows no. 4010 on Wyoming's Sherman Hill. Regarded as the longest reciprocating steam engine of ever built, the Big Boy is a direct technological descent of Robert Stephenson's *Rocket*. *Robert A. Witbeck, collection of the Center for Railroad Photography & Art*

working these big engines through its long showsheds and tunnels at high altitudes on Donner Pass, crews risked suffocation from exhaust gases and also found that it was nearly impossible to obtain a clear forward view because of accumulated smoke. By reversing the locomotive orientation, the smokebox and exhaust stack faced the tender, while the firebox rode ahead of the boiler. The locomotive was fitted with a specially designed cab with protective plates. The SP ordered fleets of Cab-Forward Mallet types from Baldwin, then later adapted the concept to a single-expansion articulated type in the 1920s (as described below).

Another extreme Mallet was the Triplex, a type first built by Baldwin in 1914 for the Erie. It consisted of three sets of running gear; two sets below the boiler and the third under the tender. In the Whyte system, the type was described as a 2-8-8-8-2. Unlike a conventional Mallet with large low-pressure cylinders fed by exhaust steam, the Triplex featured three pairs of cylinders of the same diameter: the middle engine worked high pressure steam directly from the boiler, then exhausted steam directly into the cylinders for forward and rear engines. Erie's Triplex was a curiosity but not a success. Difficulties in generating sufficient steam, chronic drafting problems owing to the tender-located exhaust for the rear-most engine, and the difficulty in balancing the output of the three sets of running gear were never adequately resolved. Erie's machines only lasted a few years in regular service, primarily working as rear-end helpers over Gulf Summit east of Susquehanna, Pa. In 1916, Virginian ordered a single Baldwin Triplex with a 2-8-8-8-4 wheel arrangement; it also suffered a short service life.

Single-expansion articulateds

In the 1920s, when railroads desired high-power locomotives that could sustain faster operation, single-expansion (simple) articulated locomotives emerged. Whereas the Mallet was designed to conserve fuel and water while operating at comparatively slow speeds, simple articulateds were designed to use high-pressure steam in both sets of cylinders. This arrangement was capable of great power and higher speeds, but required significantly more steam for sustained operation.

Improvements in two-cylinder non-articulated simple locomotives were applied to simple articulateds, namely the use of higher boiler pressure, superheaters, and larger boilers, fireboxes, and grates. Simple articulateds began appearing in large numbers beginning in the 1920s, and as the concept caught on, these locomotives were built to ever-greater dimensions.

Development and refinement of the single-expansion articulated ultimately resulted in the largest and most-powerful steam locomotives ever conceived. Chesapeake & Ohio's single-expansion 2-8-8-2 articulateds built by Alco in 1923 and 1924 were the first of these massive machines, and several railroads ordered similar large locomotives. In 1928, Northern Pacific ordered the first 2-8-8-4 Yellowstone

Articulated locomotives are built with rigid boilers. The front engine (front set of drivers) can pivot under the boiler. This is apparent on curves, as shown by Union Pacific no. 3558. This engine was built by Alco in 1923 as a 2-8-8-0 Mallet. During World War II UP rebuilt it as a simple engine. *Robert A. Witbeck, collection of the Center for Railroad Photography & Art*

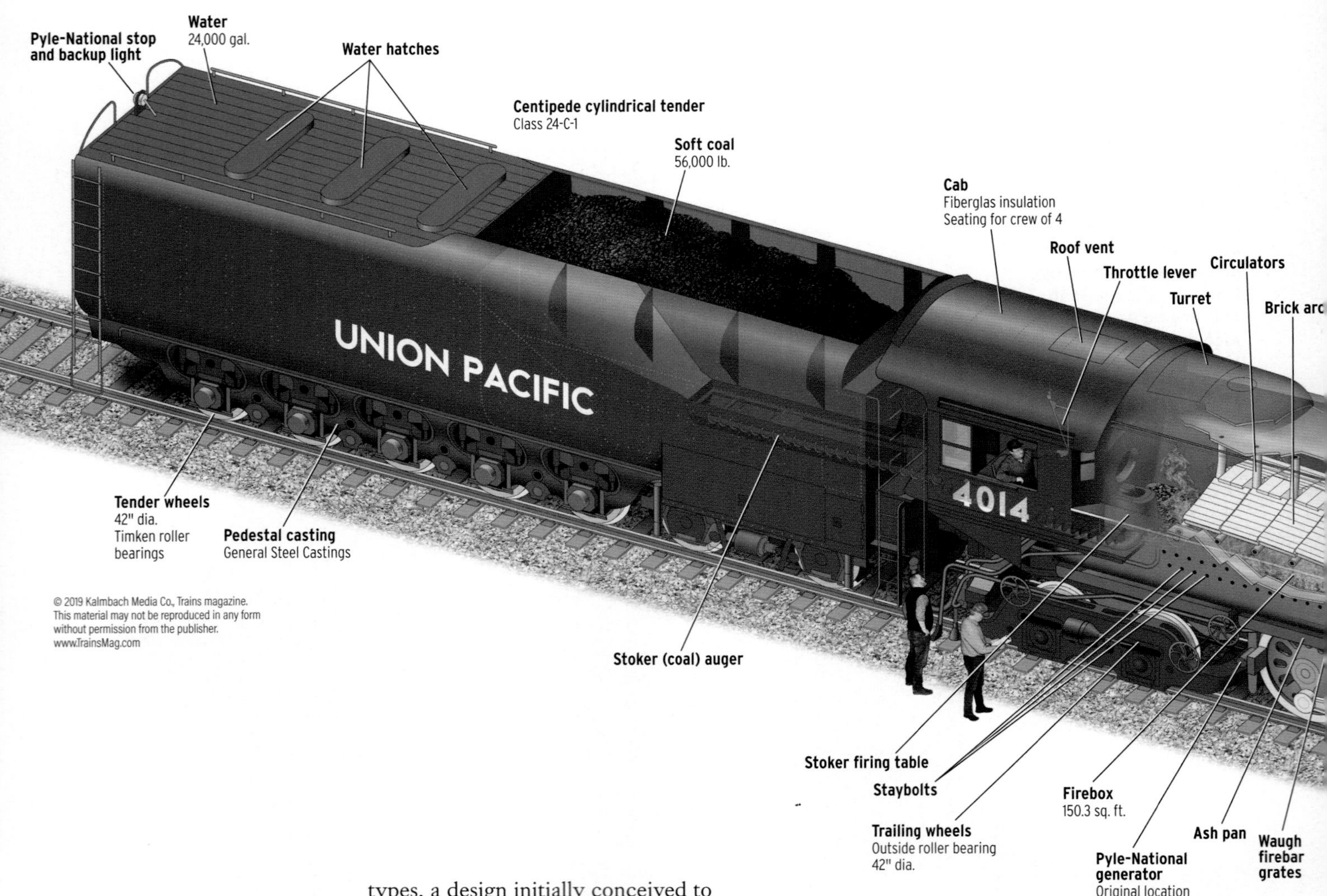

types, a design initially conceived to burn low-yield lignite as fuel. The NP's Yellowstones were the world's largest locomotives until Union Pacific's 4-8-8-4 Big Boy of 1941 and Chesapeake & Ohio's slightly heavier 2-6-6-6 Alleghany emerged in 1942.

Among the notable simple articulateds were Southern Pacific's later development of the Cab-Forward arrangement, first ordered in a simple articulated configuration in 1928. These 4-8-8-2s characterized the railroad's heavy mountain power for the next two decades. The railroad's final 4-8-8-2, no. 4294, was built by Baldwin in 1944, and it is preserved at the California State Railroad Museum in Sacramento.

The advantages offered by the simple articulated encouraged some railroads to rebuild older Mallet compounds as simple locomotives. Then, in the mid-1930s, several railroads ordered relatively fast articulated locomotives. These didn't set records for weight or size, but were remarkable machines. Norfolk & Western perfected the 2-6-6-4 type for fast freight, while in a similar effort, Union Pacific and Alco jointly developed the 4-6-6-4 Challenger, which proved to be the most widely adopted simple articulated type. The Challenger blended several technological advances with existing articulated design to produce a large locomotive that was comparatively flexible and fit clearances on most main lines. Application of a four-wheel leading truck improved the front-end stability of the articulated forward engine while better distributing the weight between the forward and rear engines. The locomotive's well-engineered suspension

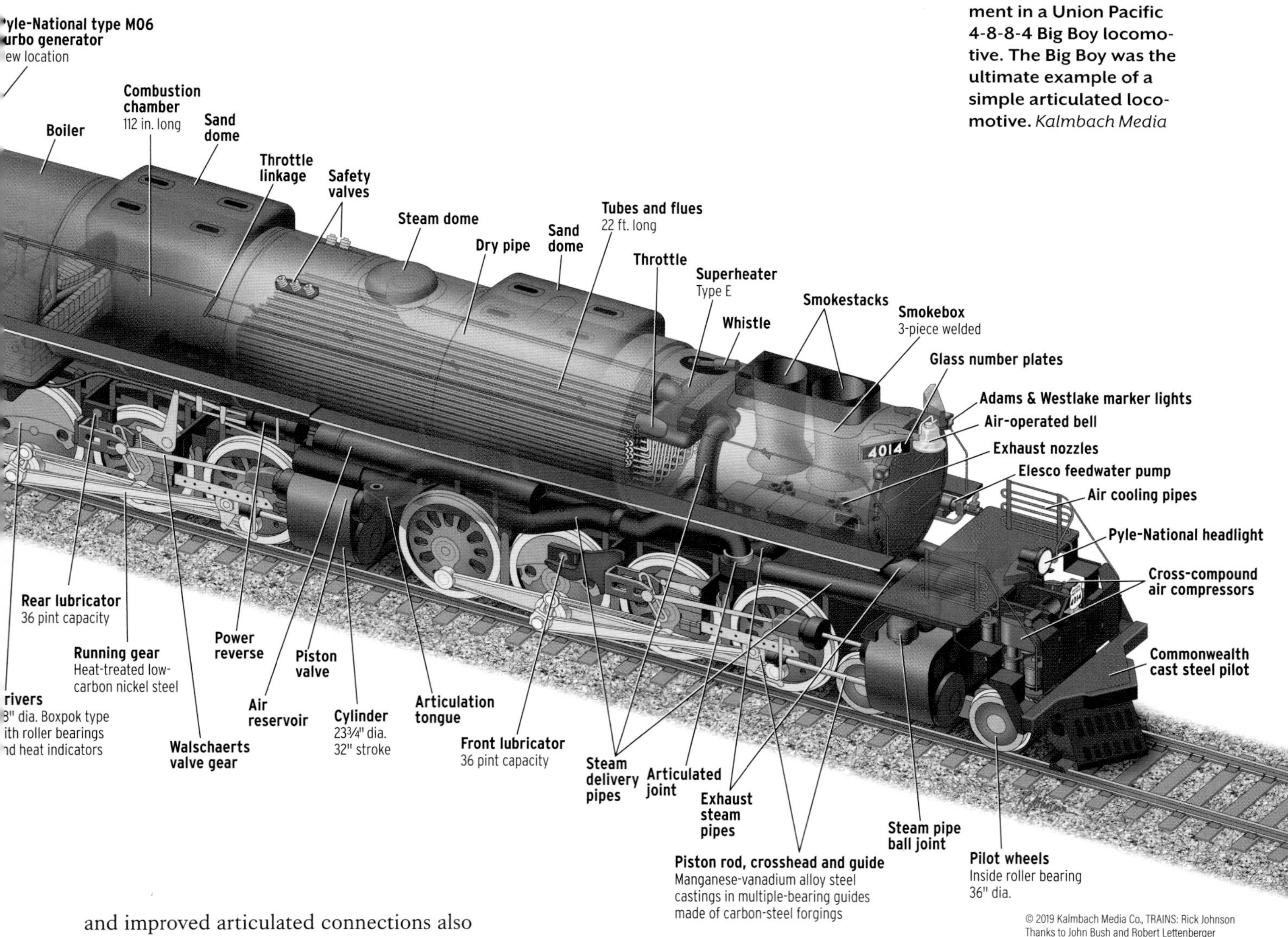

This three-dimensional cutaway view shows the arrangement of equipment in a Union Pacific 4-8-8-4 Big Boy locomotive. The Big Boy was the ultimate example of a simple articulated locomotive. *Kalmbach Media*

and improved articulated connections also aided faster speeds, and the engines pulled passenger trains as well as freight—they were capable of working up to 80 mph, although speeds of 70 mph were more practical.

The UP's massive Big Boy of 1941 essentially expanded the Challenger type with the two additional sets of drivers, one each on the rear and forward engines, along with a corresponding increase in boiler capacity. The locomotive's unusually large size and long wheelbase restricted its operating area, but it proved itself in heavy freight service, mainly hauling freight on UP's Sherman Hill in Wyoming.

Further steam development of articulated designs essentially ended by the close of World War II in 1945, with dieselization well underway.

Chapter 8

Geared, narrow-gauge, tank, and specialized steam locomotives

Shay locomotives used vertical pistons to turn a crankshaft that ran along the right side of the locomotive under the frame. They were the most-common geared locomotive, with more than 2,700 built. Western Maryland no. 6 was the last Shay built (in 1945), and the heaviest (269,960 pounds). The WM used the three-truck Shay on a steep coal-mining branch that had grades approaching 9 percent. *Western Maryland*

Along with conventional designs, builders adapted steam locomotives to specific needs and situations. These included diminutive locomotives for streetcar and elevated lines, geared (non-reciprocating) locomotives for logging and mining railroads, and various designs for 2- and 3-foot-gauge railroads.

Geared locomotives

Among the most common non-standard steam locomotives were designs using geared drive to provide high tractive effort at slow speeds on steeply graded and/or poorly built track. Geared locomotives performed jobs ill-suited to conventional rod-connected steam engines. They originated with the need to serve lumber railways that used lightly built temporary lines to reach timber stands in remote areas—track that often had undulating profiles and steep grades. Geared locomotives soon found an additional market in mining and other specialized industrial and slow-speed applications.

The three common types of geared locomotives were the Shay, Heisler, and Climax. Each differed in specific arrangement of cylinders and drive gear, but the basic principle was the same: Motion was transferred to a crankshaft and connected to driving trucks through a network of gears. This provided smooth operation (eliminating the hammering motion of side rods), power at low speeds (small-diameter wheels, with all axles powered), and the ability of the low-profile trucks to negotiate imperfections in track much better than tall, conventional driving wheels in a rigid frame.

Where conventional steam locomotives struggled on grades much steeper than 3 percent, geared locomotives could pull loads up grades of 5 percent and steeper with minimal risks from stalling. Likewise, they could work undulating tracks that might cause a conventional locomotive to derail. The trade-off was speed: geared locomotives were limited to 15 to 20 mph (but sounded like they were doing 60 when doing so).

The first commercially mass-produced—and the most common—geared locomotive was the Shay, invented by lumberman Ephraim Shay in 1878. The early Shay's arrangements consisted of a boiler on a

Lima Stone Co. no. 10 is a small (24-ton) three-truck, narrow gauge Shay built in 1925. It spent its life working the steep, uneven tracks of a stone quarry until it was retired in the 1950s. It was preserved, and is currently on display at the Allen County Historical Society Museum in Lima, Ohio, the city in which it was built. *Lima*

Climax geared locomotives are characterized by an angled cylinder at the front that turns a crankshaft located under the center of the frame. The shaft, through gears, turns all axles on the trucks. Middle Fork Railroad no. 3, a two-truck Climax built in 1913, is at Ellamore, W.V., in May 1948. *W.R. Hicks*

frame with a pair of vertically oriented cylinders situated on the engineer's side that turned a horizontal, flexible drive shaft that ran along the outside of the trucks on the right side of the locomotive. The shaft powered pivoting four-wheel trucks at each end of the locomotive through a system of beveled gears that connected to the ends of the axles. The earliest examples of the type weighed about 8 tons.

By 1885, the Shay was expanded into a more-powerful locomotive with three cylinders driving three four-wheel trucks. Most Shays were built by the Lima Machine Works of Lima, Ohio (which would later be reorganized into the Lima Locomotive Works). More than 2,700 were built. Shays were built in many sizes (from 8 to 150 tons) with two, three, or four trucks, and in standard- and narrow-gauge configurations. Lima's last and largest Shay (162 tons) was a massive three-truck locomotive built in 1945 for Western Maryland as its engine no. 6.

Along with the side-mounted drive shaft, Shays were characterized by having a boiler slightly off-center to the left of the frame (quite apparent when looking at the nose of one). The left side of the locomotive lacks a drive shaft, giving both sides very different appearances.

The Climax Manufacturing Company of Corry, Pa., began building its line of geared locomotives in 1888. These were distinguished by a pair of steeply angled cylinders positioned parallel to the boiler but inclined at approximately a 30-degree angle. The pistons had direct connections to a transverse (cross-horizontal) crankshaft that powered the trucks through networks of universal joints and drive shafts coupled with geared mesh-arrangements that powered all axles. They also varied widely in size, with some riding on three trucks. Just over 1,000 were built through 1928.

The Heisler Locomotive Works of Erie, Pa., employed similar engine design, but used angled cylinders arranged below the boiler cross-wise at 45-degree angles to the frame and facing each other in a V-arrangement. Cylinders had direct rod connections to the crankshaft, which was situated below the bottom center of the boiler (unlike the Shay, which had its driveshaft on the side). Like in the Climax, power was then transmitted to drive wheels using shafts and universal joints. However, only one axle on the inner face of each truck was engaged directly, so connecting side rods were used to couple each truck's axle pairs to power wheels on the outboard-facing axles. The Heisler type was offered in many sizes in both two-and three-truck varieties, with the largest engines weighing

Opposite top: Shay boilers are slightly offset to the left of the frame to compensate for the weight of the drive-shaft on the right side. Osborn Bay Wharf Co. no. 1 moves to couple to loads of imported lumber at the Vancouver Island (B.C.) dock in August 1961. The 30-ton, two-truck Shay was built by Lima in 1920 and acquired by OBWC in 1947; it remained in service until 1964. *John C. Illman*

approximately 90 tons. Just over 600 were built before production ended in 1941.

Following the success of these other builders, Baldwin made its own late entry into the geared-locomotive market. In 1912, it built a prototype in an effort to secure a portion the industrial/logging locomotive business. Its engine was a two-truck type with 36" wheels powered by 14x16-inch cylinders. It built just five examples through 1915.

The highly specialized service of geared locomotives meant some of them survived in service longer than conventional steam locomotives. Whereas by 1960 steam had vanished from North American mainline railroads, some geared locomotives on logging lines held on for a few more years.

Tank engines

Tank engines are steam locomotives that don't carry their water supply in a tender, instead relying on water-storage tanks applied to the locomotive itself. These are often side mounted or wrap around the top of the boiler (saddle-style). Coal is usually carried in a small bunker to the rear of the cab.

Tank locomotives were quite common in Britain, even for large road locomotives; in North America, tank engines are usually smaller switching locomotives. They're typically used in industrial and yard settings, where compact size, maneuverability, and high visibility—not to mention low initial and operating costs—are important. Many were designed for one-person operation. As switching locomotives, they don't require the large water supply of a road locomotive; when they're in a yard or industry they have ready access to a water supply if needed. Water supplies were generally 1,500-2,000 gallons, with 1 to 2 tons of coal.

The Whyte classification system applies to tank locomotive wheel arrangements, with a "T" suffix added (i.e. 0-4-0T). Standard and narrow gauge versions were built. The most common arrangements were

Hillcrest Lumber Co. no. 10, a three-truck Class C Climax built in 1928, was the next-to-last Climax built. It's working at Mesatchie Lake, Vancouver Island, B.C., in 1960. *Glenn W. Beier*

The Climax nameplate was located on the locomotive's inclined cylinder and valve arrangement. *Chris Bost*

West Side Lumber Co. no. 3 is a two-truck Heisler built in 1899 and shown working in 1963. Heislers have cylinders angled inward under the boiler, driving a crankshaft under the frame. The crankshaft powers the inward axles of each truck; side rods transmit motion to the other axles. *Glenn W. Beier*

A Brooklyn Eastern District 0-6-0T switches freight cars at Long Island City, N.Y., on November 7, 1958. Light-duty tank engines such as this one (built by Porter in 1920) carried coal in a bunker behind the cab and water on a saddle tank mounted across the boiler. This was ample fuel for short running and gave the locomotive added adhesive weight. In other respects, industrial tank switchers were primitive machines. This engine was equipped with old D-slide valves and was largely free of modern appliances.
Richard J. Solomon

0-4-0T and 0-6-0T, although larger versions were built, including some with pilot and trailing trucks.

Many tank locomotives were built by Porter and other industrial manufacturers, although major locomotive manufacturers built some as well. They are generally simple in construction, lacking modern appliances such as superheaters and feedwater heaters, with cabs featuring basic controls.

Narrow gauge locomotives

Although track gauges varied in railroading's early days, by the late 1800s the standard gauge of 4'-8½" was well established. Railroads with tighter rail spacing—known as "narrow gauge"—experienced a construction boom from the 1870s into the 1880s. Three-foot gauge was the most common, with extensive trackage in the Rockies along with lines in the Midwest and East plus many remote logging lines; 2-foot lines could be found in Maine. Although some of this track was converted to standard gauge by 1900, some narrow gauge railroads continued to operate until after World War II with a few lines still in operation.

The chief advantages of narrow gauge railroads were lower construction and operating costs. These lines permitted tighter curves and lighter roadbed; the narrower track allowed for smaller locomotives and cars, which cost less to build and required less to fuel and operate.

Narrow gauge locomotives, all but non-existent prior to 1870, presented a growing and substantial portion of the new locomotive market after 1873 with more than 20 builders engaged in narrow gauge locomotive construction. An estimated 1,400 3-foot gauge locomotives were built in the U.S. between 1870 and 1890 for common-carrier service (not including industrial engines). The most prolific builder of these was Baldwin, which by the 1870s was the largest American manufacturer of steam locomotives. During the narrow gauge boom the company built 561 narrow gauge

Number 6 is an 0-4-2T Vauclain compound tank engine built by Baldwin for the Manitou & Pikes Peak cog railway (note the rack between the rails) in 1906. Baldwin built several locomotives for the railroad, featuring saddle tanks and steeply angled boilers (to keep the boilers level on the railroad's 16 percent grades). *J. William Vigrass*

locomotives for domestic common carriers.

Before 1900, common-carrier narrow gauge locomotives were essentially scaled down versions of standard gauge designs, and other than smaller proportions they didn't require specialized designs or unusual equipment. For the most part they employed established arrangements for frames, boilers, cylinders, valve gear, and running gear, and largely used popular wheel arrangements common to standard gauge locomotives. The most-common 19th-century narrow gauge type was the 2-6-0 Mogul, with an estimated 450 of them were built to 3-foot gauge.

The trend in standard gauge steam development in the 1890s moved toward larger and more-powerful freight locomotives and faster passenger locomotives. During this time, rapid innovations in locomotive design resulted in builders introducing many improvements and new wheel arrangement.

Denver & Rio Grande was among the pioneering American 3-foot gauge lines. While the company underwent significant changes to its operations in its first few decades that resulted in changes to ownership, adjustments to its corporate name, a total refocusing on the direction of its system, and ultimately the adoption of standard gauge for its most-important routes, it also was the most-extensive and longest-lived 3-foot gauge common-carrier operation. Its first locomotives were compact Baldwin 2-4-0s, but D&RG soon acquired 2-6-0s and eventually 2-8-0s.

New England locomotive manufacturer William Mason was influenced by Britain's double-ended Fairlie locomotives—a type almost unknown in the U.S.—modifying the concept and creating a single-truck swiveling locomotive. This type became known as the Mason Bogie, and was an

Opposite top: **Hammond Lumber Company no. 17 is an example of a 2-8-2T heavy industrial tank engine. It was built by Alco in 1929 and features 44" driving wheels. As built it was oil-fired with a saddle tank over the boiler. Notice the placement of the air compressor adjacent to the smokebox (ahead of the saddle tank). The turbo-generator is positioned ahead between the smokestack and the headlight.** *Adam Stuebgen*

Wiscasset, Waterville & Farmington was one of several 2-foot gauge common-carrier railroads in Maine. This compact 2-4-4T Forney is an example of the diminutive steam locomotives that worked Maine narrow gauge lines. *Brian Solomon collection*

EORGIA
THE GOLD COA
BALDWIN LOCOMOTIVE WORKS
12
PHILADELPHIA

This narrow gauge 4-4-0 was built by Baldwin in 1876 and served California's North Pacific Coast, which connected the Bay Area with the Russian River valley. It is now among the prized displays at the California State Railroad Museum in Sacramento. It also displays an ornate, highly decorated style typical of mid-19th century wood-burning locomotives. *Brian Solomon*

early user of Walchaerts outside valve gear. Nearly 90 Mason Bogies were built for narrow gauge operations in the United States; notable operators included the Boston, Revere Beach & Lynn and Denver, South Park & Pacific. Mason Bogies were built by Mason through 1887; locomotives continued to be built to the design after that, but by other manufacturers.

A similar locomotive was the Forney, patented by Matthias Nace Forney, which featured powered axles under the boiler with a trailing truck under the tender. The Forney has drivers rigid to the frame, unlike the Mason Bogie, which has articulated drivers. Forney (author of *Catechism of the Locomotive*) was familiar to locomotive men of the 19th century for his prolific writings, knowledge, and strong opinions on locomotive design. He was among a few talented men that both invented locomotive technology and wrote about it. Later he served as the Editor of the *Railway Gazette*—one of the leading trade magazines of its day.

Forney learned the steam locomotive trade from veteran locomotive builder Ross Winans and had been in the employ of

Boston, Revere Beach & Lynn no. 14 is a 3-foot-gauge 2-4-4T Mason Bogie locomotive built by Alco in 1902. It has 49.5" drivers. The rail-road was known for its extensive fleet of Mason Bogies, including early versions built by Mason and later engines from Alco and others.
William H. Butler, Jr.

Colorado & Southern no. 60, pictured on display at Idaho Springs, Colo., is a classic narrow gauge 4-6-0 with a variety of peculiar features including an exceptionally large front plow—necessary for combating snowdrifts—and a spark arrestor on the exhaust stack designed to funnel hot cinders directly to the ballast to avoid starting brush fires. It also has a pair of air reservoirs mounted laterally atop the boiler between the steam and sand domes. *Robert A. Witbeck, collection of the Center for Railroad Photography & Art*

Denver & Rio Grande no. 463 is a class K-27 2-8-2 narrow gauge locomotive built by Baldwin in 1903. It was built as a Vauclain compound, but converted to a simple (two-cylinder) locomotive by 1909. The wheels are inside the locomotive frame, with rods and counterweights outside the frame. *Jim Seacrest collection*

Baltimore & Ohio. Forney promoted tank engine design, and his patented engine was an unusual type of tank defined by its extended locomotive frame that included a small tender and unusual 0-4-4T wheel arrangement. His one-piece locomotive plus tender was intended to provide ample fuel and water capacity, but was balanced in a way that minimized the effect of the fuel and water adding to weight on drivers. This helped eliminate a problem of other tank engines, which lost tractive effort as fuel and water were used because weight on drivers decreased. The design was built by several manufacturers. Maine's 2-foot gauge lines made the unusual choice to adapt the Forney design. In addition to the classic 0-4-4T arrangement, these railroads also bought similar locomotives with leading pilot wheels. Forney found a niche with elevated railroads, as we'll see in a bit.

20th century narrow gauge

Designing larger narrow gauge engines with substantially larger fireboxes posed special problems. Many narrow gauge railways stuck with their 19th-century antiques until their operations were abandoned or converted to standard gauge, so after 1900 there wasn't a large domestic market for new narrow gauge locomotives. Two notable exceptions were the 3-foot gauge East Broad Top in south-central Pennsylvania and Rio Grande's Rocky Mountain narrow gauge network, both of which opted to buy modern, more-capable locomotives after 1900.

The 2-8-2 Mikado type was pioneered by Baldwin in the 1890s as an export locomotive. An early buyer was Japan, which had a growing network of meter-gauge lines. The type was introduced at the time when Gilbert & Sullivan's *The Mikado,* a comic opera about the Japanese Emperor, was enormously popular, so the unusual name stuck.

Denver & Rio Grande's narrow gauge was one of the earliest domestic applications for the 2-8-2, and adaptation of this type to comply with D&RG's narrow-gauge profile helped re-define the railroad's narrow-gauge fleet in the early 1900s. Initially, it bought 15 class K-27 2-8-2s from Baldwin in 1903. These locomotives embodied several unusual features, notably an outside frame and outside counterweights and crankpins. Although new to Rio Grande, Baldwin had built outside-frame narrow gauge locomotives for export since the 1880s. In their original configuration, D&RG's class K-27s used the Baldwin Vauclain compound arrangement—making them the only narrow-gauge compounds on the Rio Grande. After a few years the K-27s were

The self-propelled steam-powered railcar was rare in the U.S. It's similar to a steam dummy, which is a steam locomotive that's disguised as a streetcar or interurban car. Pittsburgh, Cincinnati, Chicago & St. Louis no. 2 is a railcar built by Baldwin in 1898. It's powered by a 2-4-0 locomotive tucked into the right end, with a standard truck on the other end. It has 44" drivers, 140 psi boiler pressure, and is a Vauclain compound (with 9.5 x 18 and 15 x 18 cylinders). *Baldwin*

East Broad Top 2-8-2 no. 15 leads a train out of Orbisonia, Pa., in June 2009. The 3-foot-gauge Mikado was built by Baldwin in 1912. It has 48" drivers and Walschaerts valve gear. *Jim Wrinn*

rebuilt as simple locomotives. At the time of delivery, Rio Grande's K-27 2-8-2s were significantly larger and more powerful than other narrow-gauge engines, and twice as powerful as the Rio Grande's Consolidation types. They were intended to haul 220-ton trains on the railroad's steep mountain grades, but were too large for portions of the system, until the railroad upgraded clearances to accommodate them.

In 1923, Rio Grande bought a second batch of outside-frame 2-8-2s, this time from Alco, designated Class K-28. These were larger and more powerful than the K-27s. With 44" drivers the K-28s were able to work at a steady 40 mph and were preferred as passenger locomotives. In 1925, the railroad ordered its last new narrow gauge steam locomotives: 10 outside-frame Mikados from Baldwin, class K-36. However, Rio Grande's final narrow-gauge locomotives were 2-8-2s rebuilt by the railroad from old standard gauge Consolidations between 1928 and 1930.

In its early years, Pennsylvania's 3-foot-gauge, coal-hauling East Broad Top operated 2-6-0 Moguls and 2-8-0 Consolidations. But by 1911, its traffic demanded modern equipment. It invested in new steel hopper cars, and by 1920 it purchased six new 2-8-2 Mikados from Baldwin. These were equipped with modern equipment including superheaters and piston valves, and they originally used Southern valve gear, a relative rarity for narrow gauge engines—EBT's are believed to be some of the only narrow-gauge engines equipped with this type of outside valve gear. The last three engines were the biggest of its Mikados, capable of hauling 22 loaded steel coal hoppers on its ascending ruling northbound grade from the mines to Mt. Union where it interchanged with Pennsylvania Railroad.

Steam dummies

Rapid population growth of American cities in the mid-19th century saw urban transit systems searching for practical alternatives to horse-drawn trams. Horses were expensive to care for, limited hauling ability (which greatly limited the number of people transported), and were severely limited in their ability to work on hilly streets.

In the 1860s, more than two decades prior to the advent of practical electrification, street railways began purchasing small steam locomotives to haul short lightweight coaches on street trackage. This was fine in concept, but the practicality of using steam locomotives on city streets raised fears of the steam-belching engines startling horses. Tidy-conscious Victorians also frowned on unsightly locomotives that close to public view.

One compromise was to disguise locomotive in what became known as a "steam dummy" or "dummy car." To mollify complaints, small locomotives (usually 0-4-0s or 0-4-2s) were encased in horse-car-like bodies. The firebox, boiler, stack, cylinders, and running gear were carefully tucked out of sight. These small engines could tow a passenger coach or two on city street trackage at slow speeds (usually under 25 mph), and some larger versions also had room for passengers.

A Baldwin advertisement at the time described its dummy car as follows: "These machines are nearly noiseless in operation, show no smoke with the use of anthracite coal or coke, and show little or no steam

Until electrification, New York City's elevated railways operated with steam locomotives such as this 0-4-4T Forney type. The compact bi-directional Forney was ideally suited for urban elevated railway operations. The Manhattan Els were rapidly electrified with third rail beginning in 1900, thus ending the era of steam-hauled trains above New York City streets. *Brian Solomon collection*

under ordinary conditions of service. They can be run at two or three times the speed of horse cars and draw additional cars."

Steam dummies were relatively common in American cities until the 1880s, but their numbers dwindled after 1885 as the electric streetcar proved to be more efficient and cheaper to operate.

Elevated railway engines

Between 1868 and 1900, railway entrepreneurs in New York City, Brooklyn (an independent city until it was annexed by New York in 1898), and Chicago built elevated passenger railways aimed at capitalizing on urban congestion and offering an alternative to crowded city streets. Elevated lines were built on iron and steel structures above street level and were characterized by short, steep grades and tight curves. These operations required special varieties of lightweight engines with short wheelbases and comparatively high tractive effort. These engines needed rapid acceleration to travel quickly between stations—yet didn't need to attain high speeds—so typically featured very small driving wheels.

Self-contained, bi-directional tank locomotives were ideally suited for urban

Boston & Maine tank engine no. 40, built in 1895 and shown here in 1912, was one of six E1a 2-6-4T locomotives on the roster. The B&M was among several northeastern lines to use tank engines in suburban commuter passenger service. These bi-directional locomotives (note the shape of the built-on tender, which allowed vision to the rear) speeded turnaround times at the end of the run, obviating the need for turntables. *J.R. Quinn collection*

transit applications. One of the most distinctive types was patented by Matthias Forney in 1866.

Few mainline railroads placed orders for Forney's design, although a few were purchased for suburban commuter services, notably by Illinois Central. However, the Forney type was well-suited at negotiating tortuous steep elevated lines and hundreds were built for urban rapid transit service in the last decades of the 19th century.

Forney engines tended to be significantly lighter than conventional locomotives. For example, a typical Manhattan Elevated Railway Forney weighed about 15 tons, less than half the weight of a typical 4-4-0 American of the period. The elevated-service Forney engine employed unusually small cylinders (10 x 14 inches) and driving wheels (38" diameter), while burning anthracite to minimize pollution. Among the more unusual variations were Baldwin Vauclain compound Forneys built for use in Chicago.

Electrification of elevated lines put an end to these urban steam engines, many of which found work elsewhere on industrial and logging lines.

Glossary of terms

adhesion. The friction between drive wheel and rail; the ability of driving wheels to grip rails as based on the weight of a locomotive.

anthracite. Also "hard coal," known for its high heat value; slow, clean burning; and difficulty to ignite. Used as fuel by some railroads.

air brake. (see automatic air brake)

articulated locomotive. A locomotive with a hinged frame and divided sets of driving wheels.

automatic air brake. Braking system devised by George Westinghouse using a constantly charged air line throughout the train.

backhead. The rear wall of the boiler that projects into the cab.

back pressure. The force upon the piston when pressurized steam remains in the cylinder as the piston begins its return stroke.

balanced compound. A type of non-articulated four-cylinder compound locomotive featuring four cylinders in a row, with two inside cylinders driving a cranked axle and two outside cylinders driving crankpins.

bearing. A load-carrying surface that supports a turning or moving surface. See also: brass bearing and roller bearing.

bituminous. Also "soft coal"; the most-common type of locomotive fuel.

blind driver. A flangeless driving wheel, used on some long-wheelbase locomotives to provide greater ability to negotiate tight curves.

boiler. The metal pressure vessel used to convert water to steam for supply to cylinders.

boiler pressure. A boiler's maximum working pressure in pounds per square inch.

booster. A small two-cylinder steam engine attached to the trailing truck or a tender truck to supply additional tractive effort.

bore. The inside diameter measurement of a cylinder, commonly given as the first of two numbers of a given cylinder dimension (bore x stroke).

brake valve. Control valve in cab used to regulate air brakes.

brick arch. (see firebrick arch).

Bunker C. Heavy oil used as fuel for many steam locomotives (No. 6 fuel oil).

cab. The sheltered portion of a locomotive that protects the locomotive crew and controls.

Cab-Forward (or **cab-ahead**). Locomotive arrangement where cab is at the locomotive front, with the firebox and boiler trailing.

Camelback. Locomotive type with the engineer's cab moved forward to straddle the boiler, making room for a wide firebox, with a small platform at the rear for the fireman.

combustion chamber. Space between the boiler tube sheet and firebox wall, designed to facilitate more thorough fuel combustion.

compound locomotive. A locomotive that reuses steam exhausted from one cylinder to power a second cylinder.

connecting rod. (British term; see main rod)

cranked axle. Driving axle bent twice at right angles to allow a connection with a main rod to provide power.

crankpin. Short shaft anchored to a driving wheel that serves as the connection to a side rod or main rod.

cross-compound. A two-cylinder compound locomotive with high- and low-pressure cylinders on opposite sides.

crosshead. A block of metal that provides a mechanical, moving link between the piston rod and main rod.

crosshead guide. Two to four steel guide rails that hold the crosshead and allow it to slide back and forth with rod motion.

crown sheet. The sheet metal or plate forming the top of the firebox.

culm. Anthracite coal waste; sometimes used as fuel.

cylinder. Metal housing with a cylindrical opening to hold and guide the piston.

cylinder cock. Valve at the bottom of the cylinder allowing for expulsion of condensed water.

cylinder head. Metal covering that seals the end of a cylinder. The back cylinder head has an opening with a gasket for the piston rod.

D-slide valve. (see slide valve)

doghouse. Small enclosure atop some tenders to provide shelter for head-end brakeman.

driving axle. Powered axle.

driving wheel or **driver**. A powered wheel on a locomotive.

dry pipe. The pipe that carries steam from the boiler (throttle valve) to the cylinders.

Duplex. A locomotive with a divided drive (two sets of drivers) on a rigid (non-articulated) frame.

eccentric. Off-center disk connected directly to an axle or driving wheel. It connects to an eccentric rod, which may be used to pass motion to a link, rocker, or similar device in order to synchronize valve movements.

engineer. Person controlling (driving) the locomotive. Sits on the right-hand side of the cab.

exhaust stack. The locomotive chimney, located atop the smokebox at the front of the boiler.

feedwater heater. An appliance that pre-heats water before injecting it into the boiler (common makes were Coffin, Elesco, and Worthington).

firebox. The furnace, or rear enclosure in the boiler, in which fuel is burned to heat boiler water.

firebrick arch. A baffle inside the firebox composed of fire-resistant bricks that divides the firebox into two areas, one serving as a furnace and the other as a combustion chamber.

fireman. Person responsible for tending the fire and the boiler; sits on the left side of the cab.

fire tubes. Metal pipes that carry gases from the firebox through the boiler to the smokebox.

flue. A fire tube; flues are generally of larger diameter and also house piping for the superheater.

Forney. A type of tank locomotive where the engine and tender share a common frame. Patented by Matthias M. Forney.

frame. The metal structure of the locomotive carried by the running gear that supports the boiler, firebox, cab, and other upper portions of the locomotive.

fusible plug. A safety device—a metal plug device screwed into the firebox crown sheet designed to melt at a lower temperature than the crown sheet to prevent crown-sheet failure.

head-end. The front of the train; head-end crew comprises the engineer, fireman, and (sometimes) a brakeman.

helper or **helper engine**. An extra locomotive coupled to a train to assist it up a grade.

independent brake. Brake system of the locomotive only.

injector. Appliance used to force feedwater into a the boiler using a high-pressure steam jet.

Johnson bar. (see "reverse gear")

link. In a valve gear, a slotted metal component that allows for a manual adjustment to change the valve travel.

main reservoir. Primary storage tank for

compressed air on a locomotive.

main driver. The driver connected to the main rod.

main rod. The rod that transmits piston thrust (via the crosshead) to the main driving wheel crankpin.

Mallet. A four-cylinder articulated compound locomotive that features two sets of running gear under a common boiler. Named for its Swiss-born designer, Anatole Mallet (pronounced as Mal'-lay).

narrow gauge. Any rail-to-rail track width narrower than standard gauge (4'-8½"). Three- and 2-foot gauge were most common.

pilot. The leading portion of a locomotive at track level, designed to clear obstructions from the track. Colloquially known as a "cow-catcher."

piston. A disk with rod that moves back and forth (by steam pressure) within the cylinder.

piston rod. Steel rod attached to the piston that protrudes from the cylinder to provide movement; connects to the crosshead.

power reverse. Steam- or hydraulic-powered device that aids the reverse linkage in movement.

radial stay. The common boiler-firebox support arrangement used above the firebox crown sheet that features a group of staybolts to form the top arch of the boiler.

reciprocating engine. An engine (such as a steam engine) that converts energy to a back-and-forth motion.

reverse gear or **reverse lever** or **reverser**. A lever that controls the valve gear in adjusting valve travel to control the power and direction of the locomotive.

rolling stock. Freight and passenger cars.

running board. The narrow platform or walkway situated on the side of the boiler designed to allow access to boiler-mounted accessories.

running gear. The locomotive axles, springs, trucks, wheels, and associated components.

Russia iron. Highly polished rust-resistant sheet iron, popular in mid-19th century locomotive construction as semi-decorative boiler jacketing.

safety valve. Steam relief valve attached to the boiler; set to release at a point just above the boiler's working pressure.

sandbox or **sand dome**. Cylinder-shaped storage box atop the boiler that holds sand for traction.

sander. Piping and control gear that delivers sand in front of driving wheels.

saturated steam. Steam that is just above the boiling point; sometimes called "wet steam." Its temperature depends on the pressure (387 degrees F. at 200 psi).

Shay. Geared steam locomotive manufactured by Lima; named for its designer, Ephraim Shay.

side rod. Horizontal rod that connects the main driver to other drivers.

simple engine. Single-expansion (non-compound) locomotive where all cylinders receive steam directly from the boiler.

single-expansion engine. (see "simple engine")

slide valve. Traditional flat (D-shaped) valve for controlling ports to control steam admittance and exhaust from a cylinder.

smokebox. The front compartment of a locomotive boiler where spent steam is exhausted upward through the stack. The draft pulls combustion gases from the firebox through the flues.

standard gauge. Track with rails 4'-8½" apart from one another, measured at the inside face of the rails.

staybolt. Heavy threaded bolt used for supporting the inner and outer firebox plates within the boiler.

steam chest. The steam-tight box or cylindrically shaped chamber that contains the valve that controls steam admission to the cylinder.

steam dome. Protrusion at the top of the boiler where steam is collected for distribution via the dry pipe to the cylinders.

steam injector. (see "injector")

steam valve. (see "valve")

Stephenson gear. Common early type of valve gear.

stoker. Mechanical device that carries coal from the tender to the locomotive firebox.

stroke. The linear measure of a cylinder specific to distance of piston travel; the second number of a given cylinder dimension. An 18x24 cylinder has a 24-inch stroke.

superheated steam. Steam that has been raised above the temperature of the initial boiling point; also called "dry steam."

superheater. Device that circulates steam through the boiler flues to elevate its temperature (creating superheated steam) prior to delivering it to the cylinders.

switcher or **switching locomotive**. Locomotive designed for slow-speed bi-directional operation; usually lacking pilot or trailing wheels.

tank engine. A locomotive that carries its water supply on the locomotive instead of on a separate tender. Indicated by a "T" suffix when using the Whyte locomotive classification.

tender. Trailing car semipermanently coupled to the locomotive to carry fuel and water.

throttle. The valve mechanism that allows the engineer to control the flow of steam from the boiler to the cylinders.

tractive effort. Measure of force exerted by a locomotive; in the U.S., listed in pounds. Tractive effort drops as speed increases.

Triplex. A rare variation of the Mallet compound that features three sets of running gear, with the third set located below the tender.

truck. A frame used to support journals holding one or more axles. On a locomotive, a truck typically a has a swiveling frame to allow the locomotive to more easily pass through curves.

valve. Usually refers to the slide (D-slide) or piston valve attached to the cylinders to regulate steam admission. Can also refer to other adjustable devices used for controlling the passage of steam, air, or liquid through a port.

valve gear. The series of rods, eccentrics, and links that adjust the valves to regulate steam admission to the cylinders.

valve seat. The surface upon which the steam valve rests and slides upon.

valve stem. A short rod that moves the valve back and forth on the valve seat.

Vauclain compound. A specialized type of non-articulated, four-cylinder compound locomotive designed by Baldwin's Samuel Vauclain.

Walschaerts valve gear. The most-common type of valve gear; designed by Egide Walschaerts.

wheelbase. Measurement of the locomotive from the center lines of the leading and trailing drive axles (driver or rigid wheelbase) or lead pilot axle to rear trailing axle (total wheelbase). Can also include tender.

Whyte system. Method of classifying steam locomotives by number of leading, driving, and trailing wheels.

Books

1846–1896 Fiftieth Anniversary of the Incorporation of the Pennsylvania Railroad Company. Philadelphia: Pennsylvania Railroad, 1896.

A Treatise on the Locomotive and the Air Brake. Scranton, Pa., The Colliery Engineer Co., 1900.

Alexander, Edwin P. *American Locomotives.* New York, Bonanza, 1950.

Alymer-Small, Sidney. *The Art of Railroading, Vol. VIII.* Chicago, Railway Publication Society, 1908.

American Railroad Journal—1966. San Marino, Calif., Golden West Books, 1965.

Armstrong, John H. *The Railroad—What It Is, What It Does.* Omaha, Simmons-Boardman Publishing 1982.

Best, Gerald M. *Snowplow: Clearing Mountain Rails.* Howell-North Books Berkeley, Calif., Howell-North Books 1966.

Bruce, Alfred W. *The Steam Locomotive in America.* New York, W.W. Norton, 1952.

Burgess, George H., and Kennedy, Miles C. . *Centennial History of the Pennsylvania Railroad.* Philadelphia, Pennsylvania Railroad,1949.

Bush, Donald J. *The Streamlined Decade.* New York, George Braziller, 1975.

Collias, Joe G. *Mopac Power—Missouri Pacific Lines, Locomotives and Trains 1905–1955.* San Diego, Calif., Howell-North Books, 1980.

Conrad, J. David. *The Steam Locomotive Directory of North America. Vols. I & II.* Polo, Ill.: Transportation Trails, 1988.

Corbin, Bernard G. and Kerka, William F. . *Steam Locomotives of the Burlington Route.* Red Oak, Iowa, self-publishers, 1960.

Dixon, Thomas W., Jr. *Chesapeake & Ohio—Superpower to Diesels.* Newton, N.J., Carstens Publications, 1984.

Drury, George H. *Guide to North American Steam Locomotives.* Waukesha, Wis., Kalmbach Publications, 1993.

Dunscomb, Guy L. *A Century of Southern Pacific Steam Locomotives.* Modesto, Calif., self-published, 1963.

Encyclopedia of American Business History and Biography: Railroads in the Nineteenth Century. Bruccoli Clark Layman, Inc., and Facts on File, Inc., 1988.

Farrington, S. Kip Jr. *Railroading from the Head End.* Garden City, N,Y., Doubleday, Doran and Co., 1943.

———. *Railroading from the Rear End.* New York, Coward McCann,1946.

———. *Railroading the Modern Way.* New York, Coward McCann, 1951.

———. *Railroads at War.* New York, Coward McCann, 1944.

Forney, M. N. *Catechism of the Locomotive.* New York, The Railroad Gazette, 1876.

Gruber, John, and Solomon, Brian. *The Milwaukee Road's Hiawathas.* St. Paul, Minn., Voyageur Press, 2006.

Harding, J. W. and Williams, Frank. *Locomotive Valve Gears.* Scranton, Pa., International Textbook, 1928.

Harlow, Alvin F. *The Road of the Century.* New York, Creative Ave Press, 1947.

Heck, Robert C. H. *The Steam-Engine and other Steam-Motors.* New York, D. Van Nostrand Co., 1907.

Hilton, George W. *American Narrow Gauge Railroads.* Stanford, Calif., Stanford University Press 1990.

Jones, Robert W. *Boston & Albany: The New York Central in New England, Vols. 1 & 2.* Los Angeles, Pine Tree Press, 1997.

Kiefer, P. W. *A Practical Evaluation of Railroad Motive Power.* New York, Steam Locomotive Research, 1948.

Kirkman, Marshall M. *The Compound Locomotive.* New York and Chicago, The World Railway Publishing Co., 1899.

———.*Railway Equipment—The Science of the Railways.* New York and Chicago, The World Railway Publishing Co., 1903.

Klein, Maury. *Union Pacific, Vols. I & II.* New York, Doubleday & Co., 1989.

Kratville, William, and Ranks, Harold E. *Motive Power of the Union Pacific.* Omaha, Neb., Kratville Publishing, 1958.

Meyer, J.G.A. *Modern Locomotive Construction.* New York, John Wiley and Sons, 1892.

Middleton, William D. *Metropolitan Railway—Rapid Transit in America.* Bloomington and Indianapolis, Indiana University Press, 2003.

Morgan, David P. *Canadian Steam!* Milwaukee, Kalmbach Publishing, 1961.

———.*Locomotive 4501.* Milwaukee, Kalmbach Publishing, 1968.

———.*Steam's Finest Hour.* Milwaukee, Kalmbach Publishing, 1959.

Nock, O. S. *British Locomotives of the 20th Century Vol. 2.* London: Guild Publishing,1984.

Ransome, P.T.J. *Narrow Gauge Steam.* Oxford, Oxford Publishing Co., 1996.

Ransome-Wallis, P. *World Railway Locomotives.* New York, Hawthorn Books Inc., 1959.

Reagan, H. C., Jr. *Locomotive Mechanism and Engineering.* New York: 1894.

Schafer, Mike and Solomon, Brian. *Pennsylvania Railroad.* Minneapolis, Voyageur Press, 2009.

Shaughnessy, Jim. *Delaware & Hudson.* Berkeley: Howell North Books, 1967.

Shuster, Phillip, with Eugene L. Huddleston and Alvin F. Staufer. *C&O Power.* Carrollton, Ohio, Alvin F. Staufer, 1965.

Sinclair, Angus. *Development of the Locomotive Engine.* New York, Sinclair Publishing Company, 1907.

Smith, Warren L. *Berkshire Days on the Boston & Albany.* New York, Quadrant Press, 1982.

Solomon, Brian. *Alco Locomotives.* St. Paul, Minn., Voyageur Press, 2009.

———. *The American Diesel Locomotive.* Osceola, Wis., MBI Publishing, 2000.

———. *The American Steam Locomotive.* Osceola, Wis., MBI Publishing, 1998.

———. *Baldwin Locomotives.* Minneapolis, Voyageur Press, 2010.

———. *Burlington Northern Santa Fe Railway.* St. Paul, Minn., Voyageur Press, 2005.

———. *Locomotive.* Osceola, Wis., MBI Publishing, 2001.

———. *Railway Masterpieces: Celebrating the World's Greatest Trains, Stations and Feats of Engineering.* Iola, Wis., Krause, 2002.

———. *Super Steam Locomotives.* Osceola, Wis., MBI Publishing, 2000.

Solomon, Brian and Schafer, Mike. *New York Central Railroad.* Osceola, Wis, MBI Publishing, 1999.

Staufer, Alvin F. *Steam Power of the New York Central System, Volume 1.* Medina, Ohio, Alvin F. Staufer, 1961.

———. *Pennsy Power.* Medina, Ohio, Alvin F. Staufer, 1962.

———. *New York Central's Early Power 1831–1916.* Medina, Ohio, Alvin F. Staufer, 1967.

———. *Pennsy Power III.* Medina, Ohio, Alvin F. Staufer, 1993.

Staufer, Alvin F., and May, Edward L. *New York Central's Later Power 1910–1968.* Medina, Ohio, Alvin F. Staufer, 1981.

Steinbrenner, Richard T. *The American Locomotive Company—A Centennial Remembrance.* Warren, N.J., On Track Publishers, 2003.

Swengel, Frank M. *The American Steam Locomotive: Volume 1, Evolution.* Davenport, Iowa, Midwest Rail Publishing, 1967.

Vauclain, Samuel M. *Optimism.* Philadelphia, privately published, 1924.

Vauclain, Samuel M., with Earl Chapin May. *Steaming Up!* New York, Brewer & Warrren, 1930.

Walker, Mike. *Steam Powered Video's Comprehensive Railroad Atlas of North America—North East U.S.A.* Geaversham, Kent: Steam Powered Publishing, 1993.

Weissenborn, G. *American Locomotive Engineering Companion Text.* New York, c1874, reprinted by Glenwood Publishers, Felton, Calif., 1969.

Westing, Frederic. *Apex of the Atlantics.* Milwaukee, Kalmbach Publishing, 1963.

———. *The Locomotives that Baldwin Built.* Seattle, Superior Publishing, 1966.

White, John H. Jr. *A History of the American Locomotive.* Toronto, Dover Publications, 1968.

———. *Early American Locomotives.* Toronto, Dover Publications, 1972.

Williams, Harold A. *The Western Maryland Railway Story.* Baltimore, Western Maryland Railway Company, 1952.

Winchester, Clarence. *Railway Wonders of the World, Volumes 1 & 2.* London, The Waverley Book Company Ltd., 1935.

Wiswessar, Edward H., P.E. *Steam Locomotives of the Reading and P&R Railroads.* Sykeville, Md., Greenberg Publishing Company, 1988.

Wright, Richard K. *Southern Pacific Daylight.* Thousand Oaks, Calif., Wright Enterprises, 1970.

Wright, Roy V. *Locomotive Cyclopedia of American Practice, Sixth Edition—1922.* New York, Simmons-Boardman Publishing Corp., 1922.

———. *Locomotive Cyclopedia of American Practice, Tenth Edition, 1938.* New York, Simmons-Boardman Publishing Corp., 1938.

———. *1944 Locomotive Cyclopedia of American Practice.* New York, Simmons-Boardman Publishing Corp., 1944.

Brochures, Rulebooks, and Timetables

American Locomotive Company, *Louisiana Purchase Exposition*, New York City: 1904.

Baldwin Locomotive Works. *Triple Articulated Compound Locomotive for the Erie Railroad Company.* Record No. 81. Philadelphia: 1915.

Baldwin Locomotive Works. *Eight-Coupled Locomotives for Freight Service.* Record No. 99. Philadelphia: 1920.

New York Central System. *Rules for the Government of the Operating Department.* 1937

Philadelphia & Reading Railway Company and Affiliated Lines. *Rules for the Government of the Operating Department.* 1915.

Steamtown National Historic Site. *The Nation's Living Railroad Museum.* n.d.

Western Maryland Railway Company, *Rules for the Government of the Operating Department.* 1939.

Papers and Original Manuscripts

Clemensen, A. Berle. Historic Research Study: *Steamtown National Historic Site Pennsylvania.* U.S. Department of the Interior. Denver: 1988.

Chappell, Gordon. "Flanged Wheels on Steel Rails—Cars of Steamtown" (unpublished).

Johnson, Ralph P., chief engineer. *The Four Cylinder Duplex Locomotive as Built for The Pennsylvania Railroad.* Presented in New York, May 1945. Published in Philadelphia.

Johnson, Ralph P., chief engineer. *Railroad Motive Power Trends.* Presented November 1945. Published in Philadelphia.

Meyer, C. W. Comments on Ralph P. Johnson's Paper, November 29, 1945. Presented November 1945. Published in Philadelphia.

Warner, Paul T. *The Story of the Baldwin Locomotive Works.* Philadelphia, 1935.

Periodicals

Baldwin Locomotives. Philadelphia (no longer published).

Official Guide to the Railways. New York.

Railroad History, formerly *Railway and Locomotive Historical Society Bulletin.* Boston.

Railway and Locomotive Engineering (no longer published)

Railway Mechanical Engineer 1916–1952 (no longer published)

Railway Age, Chicago and New York.

Trains. Waukesha, Wis.

Vintage Rails. Waukesha, Wis. (no longer published).